D1527032

INVASION 1944
Rommel and the
Normandy Campaign

FIELD MARSHAL ERWIN ROMMEL AND LIEUTENANT GENERAL DR. HANS
SPEIDEL AT THE CHANNEL, END OF APRIL 1944

INVASION 1944

Rommel and the Normandy Campaign

BY HANS SPEIDEL

Introduction by Truman Smith,
Colonel, U.S.A. (Retired)

GREENWOOD PRESS, PUBLISHERS
WESTPORT, CONNECTICUT

This authorized translation from the original German, *Invasion 1944, Ein Beitrag zu Rommels und des Reiches Schicksal* (Tübingen und Stuttgart, Rainer Wunderlich Verlag Hermann Leins, 1949), was made by Theo R. Crevenna.

Contents

Introduction

LIEUTENANT GENERAL HANS SPEIDEL'S *Invasion 1944* tells
the story, from the German viewpoint, of one of the
most critical periods of World War II. Indeed, to most
Americans the summer months of 1944, highlighted by the
battles on the Normandy beaches, represent the climax of
the world convulsion. Every detail of this epic struggle is
today of interest not only to those Americans who participated personally in the battles on the beaches and in the
Normandy countryside, but to that still greater number
who sweated and bled in Italy, on South Pacific isles, or in
the Philippines, or were forced to stay at home. For the Norman beaches have now become a keystone in the arch of
American military tradition—worthy to stand alongside
Chancellorsville, Appomatox, Château-Thierry and the
Meuse–Argonne. Our curiosity, therefore, cannot but be
piqued as to what went on in the Château La Roche Guyon,
the headquarters of the German Army Group opposing the
Allied Normandy armies, as, day by day, American and
British pressure brought Hitler's doom nearer.

Invasion is by no means merely military history, a record
of the estimates and orders of the German Command during the Normandy struggle. This book tells a double story.

The battles are the background, while the foreground is dominated by the narrative of another climactic struggle, that between the commander of the Army Group, Erwin Rommel, "the Desert Fox," and his overlord Adolf Hitler. In *Invasion* we read how Marshal Rommel, step by step, was induced to throw in his lot with the group of generals, headed by Ludwig Beck, which was conspiring to depose Hitler—an action which was almost successful, but which finally failed on July 20, 1944, when the bomb exploding in Hitler's study in his East Prussian headquarters unfortunately and miraculously spared the Führer's life. General Speidel feels that the plot would have succeeded, despite this mishap, if Rommel had not been seriously wounded just three days previously, on July 17, by the machine-gun bullet of a low-flying Allied airplane. For, in Speidel's opinion, Rommel's prestige and powers of leadership were absolutely indispensable to the conspirators. Only his name and his voice could have induced the German people to accept a *coup d'état*.

In the fateful months just preceding and during the battle of Normandy, the struggle of wills between Hitler and Rommel took on dramatic form. Speidel's factual account of what transpired between these two men at their conference at Margival on June 17 is stuff out of which, one may be certain, dramatists of the future will fashion some new *Coriolanus* or *Wallenstein*.

The story of the generals' plot and the events of July 20 have been told superbly by Mr. Allen Dulles in *Germany's Underground*. Nevertheless, exhaustive and finely wrought as Mr. Dulles' book is, the details of Rommel's connection with the plot were not fully known in 1947 when *Germany's Underground* was published.

Still another scholarly work in English which refers in some detail to the July 20 plot against Hitler is *The Ger-*

man Opposition to Hitler by Professor Hans Rothfels of
the University of Chicago. But no matter how thorough
and careful is this fine analysis of the extent of the support
given the plotters by the German people, Professor Rothfels lacked, just as Mr. Dulles lacked, full data on the extent of Rommel's participation in the plot. *Invasion* fills
this gap.

General Speidel is probably the only man alive who can
tell the story of the Hitler–Rommel duel. He served as
Rommel's chief of staff during the Normandy crisis. Night
and day, for weeks on end, he shared the innermost thoughts
of his chief. He conducted Rommel's correspondence. He
was present at the stormy conference at Margival where
Rommel and Hitler relations reached a breaking point. He
was at his chief's shoulder when Rommel negotiated secretly with the conspirators, and records how Rommel
was persuaded to throw in his lot with the group of generals and old-line liberals who felt that Germany could be
saved only by Hitler's death.

Speidel was not a disinterested observer at these con-
spiratorial conferences. He was heart and soul a conspirator
himself and used the respect Rommel felt for his character
as well as his gifts of persuasion to induce his chief to join
General Beck and free Germany. In the end, Speidel paid
for this temerity by undergoing months of imprisonment
and torture in the notorious Gestapo prison on Berlin's
Albrechtstrasse. He carries with him the marks of the imprisonment to this day.

It has been my privilege to have known Hans Speidel
well, in the four-year period from 1935 to 1939 when I
was serving as military attaché in Berlin. He was a South
German, a Swabian, a Württemberger, a son of that German tribe in which democratic tendencies have ever been
strong. The son of a professor at the University of Tübin-

gen, Speidel acquired in his youth at the home hearth unusually broad intellectual interests which later were to prove invaluable, when his military career took forms which compelled him to grapple with political and diplomatic problems.

Although Speidel was serving as assistant military attaché to the German Embassy in Paris during the early portion of my stay in Berlin, he and I had many mutual contacts, and staff business required his frequent appearance in Berlin. In 1936 and 1937, Speidel was chief of section "West" of the German General Staff division known as "Foreign Armies," the equivalent of the American intelligence division, G-2. It was at this time that our work brought us together and we exchanged, as soldiers naturally do, military and political argument, which touched on every aspect of the then so tense European situation.

Speidel, in these years, was hoping and praying for peace, but could scarcely dissimulate his fear that Hitler's policy would bring a second world war. As French and Western specialist of the German staff, Speidel stood very close in the critical prewar years to the then Chief of the General Staff, General Ludwig Beck, later the chief conspirator in the generals' plot. It was an open secret in Berlin how bitterly Beck hated the Führer. Thus, all of us attachés knew that Speidel was in Beck's camp.

Speidel had a deep admiration for France. He had lived and traveled much in that country and had learned to understand and admire the French temperament and French ways. This feeling of attachment was to withstand even the test of a bitter war.

The author of *Invasion* had a varied war career. Duty took him to many fronts. He was present in 1940 at the "miracle" of Dunkirk, and at the subsequent battles in France which witnessed the rapid disintegration of the

French armies. From July 1940 until March of 1942, Speidel served as chief of staff of the German military government in France. This appointment was a natural one, in view of his long preoccupation with French affairs. In 1942, however, when the notorious SS took over police power in France, Speidel was transferred to the eastern front, where he participated in the Caucasus campaign and, after the tide turned at Stalingrad, in the fierce battles of 1943, which saw the German armies fighting stubbornly, as they withdrew westward towards their own frontier. On April 14, 1944, Speidel was called again to the west and appointed chief of staff of the Army Group B, whose commander, Marshal Rommel, was entrusted with the defense of the English Channel and French Atlantic coasts. Rommel and Speidel had not previously served together; neither knew the other well. Yet each rapidly acquired respect for the other's character and ability.

Speidel's forte was character. It was his inherent sense of right and wrong, as well as love of Fatherland, which caused him in 1944 to disregard his military oath of loyalty to Hitler and ally himself with the conspirators. Those who have been soldiers are aware of how sacredly the military oath is regarded in all armies—not least in our own. Speidel's decision to join the conspirators was an unusually difficult one.

Again it was Speidel's moral qualities, as well as his feeling that he was above all else a European, which caused him on August 23 to sabotage Hitler's personal orders to carry out demolitions in Paris which almost certainly would have destroyed that beautiful city. For this saving action of his, Speidel deserves the thanks not only of Frenchmen, but all mankind.

While it is natural that readers of *Invasion* will become interested in the personality of the author, particularly as he maintains his anonymity throughout by use of the third person, Speidel himself gives the center of the stage to Rommel. The Desert Fox is his hero.

Rommel proves, in *Invasion*, no unworthy hero, even under the shadow of the Normandy debacle. Both his personality and his epic achievements, first in France in 1940 and then in North Africa in subsequent war years, had previously captured the imagination of his enemies as well as his countrymen. Already, no less an Allied leader than Winston Churchill, both in speeches and in his writings, had expressed his admiration of Rommel as a worthy foe. In *Invasion* Speidel tells the story of still another epic battle of Rommel—that which took place at the conference table with his Führer, Adolf Hitler. In my opinion, his account of this strange duel will still further enhance the Rommel legend.

Speidel's story of the Normandy battle is not an exhaustive one. It is not so intended. It is rather a day-by-day notation of the successive reactions of German battle headquarters to the course of events at the front. Even this account, unfortunately, contains gaps, owing to the loss or destruction of many of the Army Group's files during the retreat from France. Nevertheless, Speidel's account of what transpired in Rommel's and Kluge's headquarters and of the German efforts to counter the gigantic Anglo-American invasion are sure to receive the careful attention of all future military historians of World War II.

Speidel's *Invasion* contains high praise of Eisenhower's unique diplomatic-military ability. A composite army of allies, history tells us, has ever been difficult to lead. Each ally has war aims of its own. National temperaments differ —often profoundly. Speidel feels that Eisenhower deserves to rank alongside Marlborough or Prince Eugene as a leader of allies.

He also has high praise for Patton's ruthless energy, his battlefield intuition, and his discernment of the points where Germany was weak. Speidel criticizes, in passing, the "methodical Allied tactics," once the amphibious operations had succeeded, and believes that with more energy and willingness to take chances, the war could have been ended by October 1944. This is a criticism we Americans can well afford to take in stride. The American Army of 1944 was both new and huge. For most units, Normandy marked their first acquaintance with the enemy.

Some readers may see in *Invasion* an attempt by the author to pin all blame for Germany's debacle on Adolf Hitler and his brother Nazis, and hence to whitewash the guilt of the German generals. That is far from my impression. To be sure, Speidel's admiration for generals like Rommel, von Falkenhausen, Stülpnagel, and Ludwig Beck is patent. Nevertheless, we should not forget that in *Invasion* he also paints unforgettable pictures of the swaggering Field Marshal Model, who, for promotion's sake, sold his soul to Hitler, and of the unstable, politically childish von Rundstedt, who, after the collapse of the July 20 plot, allowed himself to be made Hitler's instrument for punishing the conspirators.

Lastly, in a chapter which may well be regarded as an epilogue, Speidel tells the story of Rommel's murder, of the visit of Hitler's emissaries to the home of the recuperating German war hero, of the summons to accompany them, of his mysterious death, and of Hitler's incredibly strange actions thereafter.

Invasion, as an entirety, and for the various elements of which it is comprised, is worthy of being the first book by a German general on World War II to be published in America.

TRUMAN SMITH

i

THE SITUATION
IN THE SPRING
OF 1944

1

The Political Situation

BY THE YEAR 1943 Germany had passed the peak of her military strength. Disintegration was spreading through her political leadership and her military command. The Allies, on the other hand, were stiffening and unifying their conduct of the war and their political aims.

At the Casablanca conference on January 23, 1943, Roosevelt and Churchill had agreed to demand the "unconditional surrender" of Germany. An unbroken series of German political and military reverses gave the Allies encouragement and confidence in victory: the Stalingrad disaster in February 1943, the capitulation in May of the German-Italian army in Tunisia, the loss of Sicily and the overthrow of Mussolini in the summer, the landing of the Allies on the Italian mainland in September with the ensuing capitulation of Italy, and finally the collapse of the U-boat and Luftwaffe offensives. These events also served to draw the Anglo-Saxon powers into a constantly closer alliance with the Soviet Union.

As a matter of fact, Roosevelt, Churchill, and Chiang Kai-shek had agreed in Cairo on November 1, 1943, on a campaign through the Balkans with the twofold purpose of defeating Germany and preventing the Red Army from overrunning Central Europe. However, at the Teheran conference on December 1, 1943, Roosevelt and Churchill yielded to the wishes of Joseph Stalin. They agreed to start a "second front," not in the Balkans but by invading France, as a necessary prelude to decisive operations reaching into the heart of Germany. It is not yet clear whether the American wartime leaders failed to recognize the political significance of a Balkan operation, or gave way in order to allay Soviet distrust of Great Britain's intentions. In either case, when the Allies renounced their Balkan plans, they substantially modified the outcome of the war and determined the political alignment that was to evolve in the years after the war. With the help of the Anglo-Saxon powers, Stalin established his claim to the "heritage of the Hapsburgs."

Another agreement of the highest importance resulted in the appointment on December 24 of General Eisenhower as Supreme Commander of the Allied land, sea, and air forces for the invasion of Europe. Since 1942 a small staff of British and American officers in England had been developing plans for the invasion.

The German government quickly learned the results of the Teheran conference, but Hitler did not take them seriously enough. In the spring of 1944, the general situation could be summarized as follows:

Italy had been eliminated from the war. On April 1, 1944, Hitler described the defection of Italy as "a concentration of forces and strengthening of the German position."

Spain's agreement of February 10, 1943, to defend her neutrality was in fact of no importance to Germany.

Hungary, under the leadership of Admiral Horthy, had

put out feelers to the Western powers through her minister in Lisbon for an armistice or a separate peace treaty. When Hitler learned of this, he forced Horthy to accept a new government under Stojay, the former Hungarian minister in Berlin. But even the Stojay government was not subservient enough for Hitler; in October 1944 he arranged for it to be overthrown by Salassy and had Horthy arrested.

In the Balkans, Bulgaria had been deprived of its leadership by the "elimination" of King Boris.

The eastern territories of Rumania had become a battlefield after superior Russian forces had broken through the two German southern army groups and had pushed them back into Bessarabia.

In June 1943, Turkey had sent a military mission of high-ranking officers to the Führer's headquarters and to the eastern theater of war to study the military and political situation. By the spring of 1944, however, Turkey was more and more obviously taking sides with the Allies. The German flank in the Near East no longer seemed secure.

Hitler expected only indirect help from Japan. He had rejected the idea that Japanese forces could be brought to bear against the Soviet enemy on the European front.

All of Hitler's hopes emanated from his expectation that the coalition between the Western powers and Soviet Russia would fail and that Great Britain would collapse from "moral exhaustion." Hitler believed that he could give the *coup de grâce* to the Anglo-Saxon will to wage war by the sudden use of his "miracle weapon."

Under these circumstances the political situation precluded any possibility that Germany could bring the war to a victorious end. It was also clear that even a stalemate could not be achieved under the leadership of Adolf Hitler.

2

The Military Situation

THE MILITARY situation was as gloomy as the political
situation. The time was past when a purely military
leadership could achieve victories systematically and in
a soldierly fashion, as in Poland in 1939 and in France in
1940. In the west, Wehrmacht forces now waited along the
new "Great Wall," the Atlantic Wall, for an invasion by
the Allies. These defense forces were inadequate in numbers, poorly organized, and deficient in modern weapons.

Africa and the Mediterranean were lost; the enemy was
methodically pushing the German front in Italy ever
further northward.

In the east, Hitler had begun his campaign on the Russian front with no single objective, with no main effort.
The offensives of the three army groups were launched
against the Ukraine with its industrial basins of Stalino and
Kharkov; against Moscow; and against Leningrad. The
offensives to the north and the center bogged down without reaching their objectives.

In 1942 Hitler had ordered simultaneous operations
across the lower Don towards the Caucasus, to seize the

Poti-Baku line, and across the upper Don towards the Volga and Stalingrad. The forces employed were inadequate. Disregarding the teachings of Clausewitz, the German armies attempted to capture a geographical area, rather than to destroy the enemy armies. The Soviet armies withdrew with great skill. The Chief of the General Staff of the German Army, Colonel General Halder, was held responsible for these mistakes and was dismissed in September 1942.

After the strategy of 1942 had failed, Hitler, in the struggle to capture Stalingrad, entrusted the protection of the vulnerable German flank at the Don to his allied contingents (the First Rumanian Army, the Eighth Italian Army, and the Second Hungarian Army), which lacked both modern equipment and the will to fight. The capture of Stalingrad was made impossible by the unwise combination of these forces and the severity of the Russian winter.

The disaster of Stalingrad was not inevitable; Hitler simply was not able to modify his political and propaganda line, nor was he able to learn from experience. Also General Paulus, the commander of the German Sixth Army, could not decide promptly enough to withdraw on his own responsibility while fresh divisions were still available to cover a retreat.

In 1943, after the successful German counteroffensive in March on Kharkov and Byelogorod, Hitler ordered the summer offensive with the code name "Citadel." "Citadel" was aimed from the Byelogorod and Orel areas at cutting off the Kursk salient, drawing the enemy out and stifling the expected offensive before it could get under way.

"Citadel" could have succeeded only if it had followed immediately upon the Kharkov-Byelogorod counteroffensive of March 1943—the last successful *retour offensif*. The failure of Operation "Citadel" brought about the final military phase: the Russian counteroffensive set in and was intensified, with only slight interruptions for regrouping and supply, until the catastrophe of 1945. Hitler described this Russian operation as a *"guerre d'usure"* or blood-letting for the Soviet Union. There is no need to call attention here to the immense resources of Russia at that time.

Hitler had ordered that the Dnieper River not be fortified, "because otherwise the army would be peering over its shoulder and would not hold the front line," in the belief that a more successful defense could be achieved on some rearward fortified line. This order emanated from his surly mistrust of the front-line troops. Despite the repeated proposals of the General Staff, there was no advance planning, no preparation of fortified lines to the rear. Such defensive positions were already lacking during the first winter of the Russian campaign, 1941–42. The psychology of Hitler explains why these preparations were omitted in the west as well.

Two German corps were in danger of being surrounded near Cherkassy in January-February 1944, and the Army High Command demanded that these troops be withdrawn. Hitler ordered them to hold their ground without retreat. He thought that he would be able at a later date to use the Cherkassy-Korssun area for operations against Kiev "to cause the collapse of the Russian front." There might have been a fatal catastrophe in the Cherkassy pocket but for the fact that the local army command had already ordered the two corps to fight their way out days before the reluctant permission to retreat was received from Hitler and the High Command. That is how it was possible to save at least 35,000 out of 54,000 men.

In the spring of 1944 the Seventeenth German Army was engaged in a death struggle in the Crimea. This army could have been saved if the peninsula had been abandoned in time. Even as late as January 1944, Hitler believed that he could hold the narrowed Sevastopol bridgehead, which was surrounded and besieged, and that he must do so for the political effect that it would have upon Turkey. Fragments of the Sixth Army retreated, fighting severe rearguard actions through Odessa until they reached the Rumanian frontier. The Eighth Army, under Infantry General Otto Woehler, fighting in a forward position between the Bug and Dniester rivers, retreated "like a wounded lion," while a much superior enemy force tried to press back its north flank and surround the First Panzer Army.

A timely retreat from Bessarabia and the preparation of a defensive line along the Pruth River with the Carpathian Mountains as the pivot, were proposed to Hitler. This temporary solution could have provided a breather while over-all strategical decisions were being made, but he rejected it.

Field Marshals von Kleist and von Manstein, formerly supreme commanders of the Central "A" and Southern Army Groups, were replaced on March 31 by the newly promoted Colonel General Schörner and Field Marshal Model.

On the Central and Northern Army Group fronts, there was a deceptive calm except for local skirmishes. At that time reports reached the Führer's headquarters of large-scale Soviet preparations to attack the Central Army Group.

Adolf Hitler did not see, or did not want to see, the vital problems on the eastern front on January 1, 1944. The possible loss of the Russian hinterland would deprive Central Europe of a large proportion of the food and raw materials which these areas supplied.

Even outsiders could notice the tension prevailing in the

headquarters of the High Command. The Chief of Staff of the Army, Colonel General Zeitzler, who was responsible for the eastern front, and his assistants walked out of the Berchtesgaden conference room when Generals Jodl and Warlimont began discussion on the "OKW" fronts—Norway, Finland, the west, the Mediterranean, and the Balkans. The dualism in the High Command of the Wehrmacht (armed forces) and the High Command of the Army had its origin in the mind of Hitler. The Chief of the Wehrmacht Command Staff in the High Command of the Wehrmacht, Colonel General Jodl, under the immediate influence of Hitler, directed all operations in these war theaters, whereas General Zeitzler, Chief of Staff of the Army, with the army apparatus at his command had to be content with the eastern front only. He was nicknamed the "East Chief" and had lesser powers of decision than Hindenburg and Ludendorff had in the first year of World War I. This division in the Supreme Command led to daily friction and seriously damaged the conduct of the whole war. This became especially evident after June 20, 1944, when the Soviet summer offensive against the Central Army Group started.

Further confusion of military leadership resulted from the conflicting aims and demands of Admiral Dönitz for the Navy and Marshal Göring for the Air Force. From the spring of 1943 on, U-boat warfare showed itself to be increasingly ineffective and the naval losses could no longer be replaced. The Luftwaffe never recovered from the bloodletting that it sustained in the Battle of Britain.

Early in 1944, therefore, the military situation was not very hopeful. But the fronts in the west, the south, and the east were still holding and a military catastrophe had not yet occurred.

3

The Situation within the German Armed Forces

Heavy military and political stresses had fundamentally altered the structure and inner cohesion of the German armed forces.

Hitler had assumed supreme command of the Wehrmacht on August 2, 1934, upon the death of President von Hindenburg. He had defined his own responsibilities in a letter of August 20 to the minister of war, Colonel General von Blomberg, in these terms:

"Today after the law of August 2 has been confirmed, I want to thank you and the Wehrmacht for the oath of loyalty taken to me, your Führer and supreme commander. Just as the officers and soldiers have sworn loyalty to the new state in my person, I will always regard it as my highest duty to protect the standing and integrity of the Wehrmacht at all times. In fulfillment of the testament of the immortal Field Marshal [von Hindenburg] and true to my own will, I want the army to remain the sole bearer of arms in the nation. Adolf Hitler, Führer and Reich Chancellor."

Until February 4, 1938, he more or less kept the promise
that he had also given Reich President von Hindenburg,
and resisted political penetration of the army. He also with-
held his opinions in all military matters during the first
years after assuming power.

The bid for power by the SA, Hitler's brown-shirted
storm troopers, was foiled by the events of June 30, 1934.
But the Reichsführer of the SS, Heinrich Himmler, began
in 1937 to arm certain SS units. This led to the dualism of
the army and the SS forces, and a demand by the SS for
political and military leadership. Hitler had broken his
word to "the sole bearers of arms."

Upon the SS forces were conferred the privileges of a
Praetorian Guard, and they were thought of as the future
standing army in peacetime. The strength of this state
within the state, this army within the army, was at the end
of the war, 700,000 men.

The predominance of the traditional school in the army
ended on February 4, 1938, when Hitler assumed control
of the High Command of the armed forces, following an
attempt by Himmler to defame the Commander in Chief,
Colonel General Baron von Fritsch. Regrettably, there developed among the military leaders a dangerous tendency
towards self-effacement.

But the military leaders of Germany were children of
their times, and like many others in public life, they did
not see everything that later became apparent to them. The
traditional virtues of the Army were cleverly and un-
scrupulously misused to an ever increasingy degree. Only
Colonel General Ludwig Beck, in 1938, repeatedly risked
his position and his own person to oppose the fateful ma-
neuverings of a head of state who was willing to risk all.
But Hitler's successes in foreign relations at Munich,

in which he was aided by the Allies, deprived Beck and Halder, his deputy and successor, of their weapons.

After the war had begun, and especially after 1941, Hitler sought to make a "political organization" of the army. Its strength had hitherto consisted in its being impervious to all party influences, and in its unselfish service to the Fatherland. But now some of the military leaders began to acknowledge Hitler's prestige, particularly after the successful campaigns in Poland, Norway, France, and the Balkans. The cult of "the greatest general of all times" began to take hold.

Hitler and Goebbels made cunning use of these mass-psychological moments and worked for "revolutionary militarism." The result was that a number of officers, intoxicated by Napoleonic dreams, became merely service office holders. It had previously been the custom of the army to follow the advice of Washington: "Take only gentlemen for your officers."

The majority of officers of all ranks, particularly officers of the General Staff, were secretly against the political penetration of the army, which they thought would weaken the reliance of the troops on their officers. They opposed the military "leadership" of Hitler. The arbitrary and extravagant mentality of Hitler found expression in preposterous orders to his commanders and in interference with the military courts. A new suprise in the winter of 1943–44 was the introduction of National Socialist political officers, party men in military uniform, whose duties compared with those of the commissars in the Red Army. Thus Hitler was guided by the Russian example and not by Carnot, who, when the armies of the French revolution were created by the *levée en masse*, strove to avoid political indoctrination of the French army officers.

As the army was drawn into the labyrinth of party pol-

itics, as its loyalty and faith were destroyed by the National
Socialist political officers, and as authority itself was under-
mined, the inner structure and the outward prestige of the
army became brittle. "Unreliable officers" were dismissed,
and the principle of giving freedom, even in the military
sense, to a responsible person was abandoned—a principle
which had been valid since the times of Frederick the
Great. In the end such a man as Heinrich Himmler became
an Army Group Commander. Military knowledge and
ability, and especially feelings of a moral responsibility to
God and the Nation, began to dwindle.

Military leaders who evidenced a humanitarian attitude
were no longer effective. Such lucid spirits as the Chief
of the General Staff, General Ludwig Beck, were placed
on the retired list, and thus eliminated.

As in other armies of our and previous times, the military leaders of all ranks fell into three groups: the ordinary
soldiers, who obeyed blindly, who were credulous and in-
dolent; the ambitious party soldiers with an eye to promotion; and the thinking soldiers, whose guiding principle
was patriotism.

A sociological and psychological examination of the character and spirit in which these groups behaved must be left
to a later investigation; only a few words shall be added
here about the third group.

A significant number of the officer corps, principally the
General Staff officers, had disapproved of the internal and
external policy of Hitler before the war. Although they
must be adjudged guilty of the sin of omission—for example, the silent acceptance of the murder of General von
Schleicher and General von Bredow on June 30, 1934—
they did attempt to intervene in 1938.

But when General von Fritsch and General Beck had
been removed, there was revealed not merely a loss of will

to oppose Hitler—the means and the opportunity for opposition seemed to be lost as well. Up to the end of 1937 the people and the Army were convinced and agreed with such demands as Hitler had made, since they were to have been realized without recourse to war. After the undeniable success of Hitler at Munich, a pact of friendship was concluded with France on December 6, 1938. Very few guessed how much inner corruption and outward hypocrisy had taken hold. Very few guessed that Hitler would not keep his promise and actually wanted war.

During the war the problem became even more difficult for the German generals. Practically all the troops fought well at the front. It would be factually wrong and politically shortsighted to deny to the German soldier that measure of respect which civilized nations have always accorded even to the enemy. The opinion of world history has usually disregarded the momentary tendency to condemn a defeated enemy. No one thought of calling to account the soldiers of the religious wars of the sixteenth and seventeenth centuries. No one indicted the marshals, officers, and men of Napoleon and of France, although Napoleon was decried as an aggressor by the coalition. The mass executions by the Duke of Alva in 1568 and the behavior of the northern states after the American Civil War are only exceptions to the rule. An officer corps that had been developed to serve a monarchist form of government was not adaptable to an eventual *coup d'état* or even to a critical attitude towards the head of state. This was a source of strength as long as the Army was commanded by a monarch responsible only to God. It was weakness when a godless man assumed control of the Army's destiny.

The officer corps of the Reichswehr had been purposely kept unpolitical after 1920, because the structure of the state and the security of its rulers demanded it. Remaining aloof from political affairs did not lead to a clear separation of party politics and essential policy. Thus the officer corps remained inexperienced in political matters and lacked an ability to form sound judgments.

The highest commanders in time of war have not always been able to differentiate between the obedience due to God and conscience and the obedience due to men. This uncertainty is not peculiar to Germany.

To refuse to obey orders and to conspire against the regime presupposed a special insight and foresight in the minds of the senior officers—that and a "metaphysical civil courage."

A decision would have been easier for our best military commanders had it not been for the agreement at the Casablanca conference to demand "unconditional surrender." This created a psychological obstacle which any soldier would find difficult to evaluate.

ii

APPRAISAL
OF THE SITUATION IN THE WEST
PRIOR TO THE INVASION

1. ROMMEL'S HEADQUARTERS, CHÂTEAU LA ROCHE-GUYON ON THE SEINE

2. Rommel and His Staff at the Channel, End of April 1944

1

The Status of the Enemy

THE NEWLY appointed Chief of the General Staff of Army Group B, Lieutenant General Dr. Hans Speidel, was questioned at Berchtesgaden on April 1, 1944, as to whether the Western Allies would make any attempt at a large-scale invasion. The Commander in Chief of Army Group B, Field Marshal Rommel, and his staff never doubted that such an invasion was imminent and could decide the whole war.

There were about 75 divisions in Great Britain, of which the Army Group believed 65 were composed of fully trained officers and men of the younger age groups. These divisions had received special training, and could be used at short notice for landing operations. There were between 40 and 45 British and 20 to 25 American divisions. All were largely motorized or mechanized, and there were among them seven airborne divisions. The invasion forces under the supreme command of General of the Army Dwight D. Eisenhower consisted of the Twelfth Army Group of General Omar N. Bradley, with the First and Third U.S. Armies under General Courtney H. Hodges and General

George S. Patton; and the Twenty-first British Army Group of Field Marshal Sir Bernard Montgomery, consisting of the First Canadian and Second British Armies commanded by General H. D. G. Grevar and General Miles C. Dempsey.

If anyone still doubted whether an invasion was intended, the news received in March 1944 should have been enough to dispel all doubts. Some of the very best British and American divisions embarked from southern Italy and the Mediterranean for the United Kingdom—the 1st and 7th British Armored divisions, the 1st British Air-borne Division, the 51st British Infantry (Highland) Division, the 1st and 9th American Infantry divisions, and a special landing unit. A large number of landing craft and other ships was likewise transferred.

The main effort of the war was thereby shifted from the Mediterranean to the British Isles; Italy became a secondary theater of war. The weapons and equipment of the Allied divisions were excellent. They had the most recent technical devices: artificial harbors to make the landings independent of the long-established ports of the western seaboard; steel-mesh rolls to transform meadows into serviceable airfields in a short time; a pipe line to pump fuel across the Channel, so that this vital supply problem was solved; new steel bridging sections to make it possible to overcome speedily and securely any water barriers and terrain obstructions.

The navies of the United States and the British Empire were assembled in the harbors of the British Isles. The tonnage available was sufficient to transport twenty divisions simultaneously. A rapid shuttle service between loading and unloading points could be achieved because of the short distance involved and because adequate air protection could be maintained at all times.

The seventeen thousand first-line aircraft of the Allies could simultaneously carry out strategic bombing of Germany and support the landing operations on the French coast.

The Allies possessed an intelligence network that had been built up and tried in peacetime. It reinforced and gave impetus to the French resistance movement. Although these underground forces had been increasing their activities since the winter of 1943–44, they were of no great importance north of the Loire. There was no sabotage on a large scale anywhere until the spring of 1944.

All indications of imminent invasion were watched by Army Group B with greater attention after the intensified air offensive began at the end of April 1944. They were carefully registered and plotted on their staff maps.

Flights into the interior, bomber raids, feint or mock attacks by Allied naval craft, mine-laying, mine-sweeping, acts of sabotage by the resistance—all these seemed to point to an intention to land in the area between the Somme and a St. Mâlo-Orléans line.

It was difficult to assess the enemy potential because the Army Group received its intelligence material in predigested form from the following authorities: the Commander in Chief West (von Rundstedt), the High Command of the Army (von Zeitzler), the G-2 section of the General Staff of the Army, and the High Command of the defense forces, or Wehrmacht (Hitler-Keitel). The Commander in Chief West by means of a standing order had forbidden the Army Group to work directly with the German Intelligence Service (*Abwehr*), which had to report to the High Command of the Wehrmacht. The Army Group had, for instance, no information on the resistance forces in France, and knew nothing about their role in case of an Allied invasion. The Army Group received its reports second hand, and there was not a single trained intelligence officer at Army Group Headquarters.

The Army Group was forced to gather its own military and political intelligence secretly. Even the Field Marshal was not kept officially informed of the course of operations in Italy and on the eastern front. It was only through his personal connections that he was able to keep in touch with the situation on other fronts. Consequently, the telephone and other means of communication could be used only with the greatest caution.

The lack of information made itself felt after D Day, when the Army Group had to assess the likelihood of a second landing. The High Command of the Armed Forces (Wehrmacht) failed to provide information on the technical development of weapons, such as the progress and probable effectiveness of V-bombs, atomic developments, special naval weapons, and jet fighter planes.

When, by the end of April, the Allies seemed to have their three services in readiness in the British Isles, our principal interest was to determine the probable date of the invasion. There were restrictions on travel in the British Isles, and British industry complained when the Home Guard was called up. The most ominous sign was the intensified air offensive, which indicated an imminent attack, although its exact timing would depend upon weather conditions. The High Command of the Wehrmacht, upon advice from the German Navy, named May 18 as the certain date for the beginning of the invasion. This "zero day" came and went, and the Naval Command in the west then expected the attack to take place not before August.

Field Marshal Rommel expected invasion daily and prepared his troops for it. He was thankful, however, for every delay that gave him more time for political and military preparations and for improving the defensive power of his men. He suggested repeatedly that the Allied concentrations be reconnoitered, attacked, and harassed. His intention was that U-boats should attack the British harbors, that controlled mine fields should be laid—but Hitler did not permit production of the type of mine which Rommel proposed—that there should be bomber attacks on the Allied staging areas, with their masses of men and matériel, and that V-1 rocket bombs should be launched against England. However, production of the V-1 bomb encountered delay after delay.

The Field Marshal assumed in April 1944 that the invasion would be directed against the mouths of the Somme, Bresle, Arques, and Seine, with their harbors of Abbeville and Le Havre, the coast of Calvados and the Cotentin peninsula with its port, Cherbourg. At this time he considered it vital to the Allies to capture a sizable port at an early stage. It was impossible for him to realize the importance of the artificial harbor which was to spring into being in June on the coast of Calvados.

Allied air supremacy had to be assumed under all circumstances.

The German Navy did not think it possible for landings to be made in the mouth of the Seine or along the Calvados coast. They thought it improbable that the enemy would risk a landing on the Calvados coast, particularly because of its rocky shallows. For this reason the coastal defenses in this part of Normandy were inadequate.

Intelligence reports confirmed the importance of the Normandy coast as an invasion target, and, at the beginning of May, Rommel demanded that the III Flak (antiaircraft) Corps, scattered over the whole of central and northern France, be concentrated and put under his command. Its four regiments and twenty-four up-to-date batteries would have provided considerable fire power for aircraft and tank defense, between the Orne and Vire rivers. Göring turned down this request.

At the end of May the Navy sent a few antiaircraft ships —improvised coastal vessels with antiaircraft guns mounted on them—to the waters surrounding the mouth of the Vire.

Field Marshal Rommel, unlike Hitler, did not expect a landing on the Channel coast at Cap Gris Nez. After the beginning of May his impression was that the enemy would not ram his head against the hardest spot in the defense just for the sake of a short sea voyage and short supply lines. He thought Brittany to be an unlikely invasion area, in spite of its favorable harbors, because the terrain would restrict operations after landing.

The Army Group was skeptical about the High Command view that the Allies would attack in strength on the coast of Belgium at the mouth of the Scheldt. This did not seem likely, since the main shipping concentrations were in south-coast ports, in western England, and in Wales. The pattern of Allied air activity could not be interpreted as preparing for landings so far north.

Field Marshal Rommel believed that several landings would take place simultaneously or in rapid succession in areas that were linked in the Allied plan of operations. He believed also that the possibility of a feint landing should be taken into account. The coast between the Somme and the Bay of St. Mâlo, he thought, was the most dangerous sector.

There were reports from outside Rommel's command that landings might take place on both banks of the Gironde estuary and also on the Mediterranean coast of France. The Army Group did not consider a landing in the Bordeaux area likely, but thought an invasion on the Mediterranean coast of France, followed by a push along both banks of the Rhone, probable but of secondary importance. It might

be aimed at taking the German Atlantic defenses in a
pincers movement; therefore, it was examined in the course
of operational studies.

The Field Marshal assumed that the over-all operational
plan of the Allies would call for making the Paris area their
first target, after a successful landing either north or south
of the Seine, cutting off Brittany. From there they would
advance with concentrated forces against Germany. He
thought it vital to the Allies for operational, political, and
psychological reasons to seize the Paris area.

2

The German Command
and the German Forces
in the West

HITLER'S DIRECTIVE to the western command was: The decisive action must be fought along the Atlantic Wall itself. The defense must be conducted on the coast as the main line of resistance, and this line must be held at all costs. The enemy invasion attempts are to be broken up either before or during the landing operations, and local lodgments of enemy forces are to be destroyed by automatic counterattacks.

There was to be no strategical maneuvering on the western front; the order was to hold every inch of ground. The Staff was forbidden in its operational planning to make provision for the enemy's probable movements in the interior of France after a successful landing.

Free processes of thought were thus banned. The Germans had learned in other theaters of war—Russia and Africa—that freedom to operate strategically could be abandoned only at heavy cost to themselves.

When the British Army was defeated on the Continent and withdrew from Dunkirk in June 1940, Britain made plans for defense in depth of her island against German invasion. These plans evolved under the leadership of Winston Churchill.

THE CHAIN OF COMMAND

The chain of command in western Europe conformed neither to the timeless laws of warfare nor to the demands of the hour nor even to common sense. Hitler thought that he could apply his revolutionary principle of divided responsibilities to the conduct of war and play off one commander against another to his own advantage. This not only led to confused leadership, but also made the system of command chaotic. Under the Commander in Chief for the West (Field Marshal von Rundstedt) there were Army Group B (Field Marshal Rommel) in the Netherlands-Loire sector and Army Group G (Colonel General Blaskowitz) in the Loire-Spanish frontier-Mediterranean coast-Alps sector.

The western naval command (Admiral Krancke) received orders direct from the German Naval Staff, while the Third Air Fleet (Field Marshal Sperrle) received orders from Göring. Thus, operations at sea and in the air could be directed or co-ordinated neither by the Commander in Chief for the West nor by the commander of Army Group B. The military commanders were only partially informed of the operational intentions of the other two services, and usually too late. They could make requests without assurance of their fulfillment.

Field Marshal Rommel had been given the additional mission from the Führer of examining the entire western front from Denmark, via the Bay of Biscay, the Pyrenees, and the Mediterranean, to the Alps. He was expected to

test the state of defenses and unify measures of defense.
He possessed no authority to give orders but had the duty
of reporting direct to Hitler or to the High Command of
the Armed Forces (Wehrmacht), keeping the Commander
in Chief in the West informed of his reports.

The military governors of France (Infantry General
Karl Heinrich von Stülpnagel), of Belgium and northern
France (Infantry General Alexander von Falkenhausen),
and of the Netherlands (Air General Christiansen) were
subordinate to the Commander in Chief West in military
matters, but in all matters of administration and exploitation
of their areas for the war effort, they were directly responsible to the High Command of the Wehrmacht. Since
early 1942 higher SS and police officers of the Security
Service (Secret Police) exercised the executive power in
the occupied territories. They received their orders direct
from Himmler—orders which were kept secret from the
military governors. Thus, the Commander in Chief West
was usually confronted with accomplished facts, even in
such serious matters as deportations and executions.

The higher SS and police leaders also watched the activities of the Wehrmacht through their special agents.

German political difficulties in France were aggravated
by the rivalries of party officers and the SS. The German
Embassy in Paris under Ambassador Abetz was in itself an
anomaly, as no state of peace had been declared between
Germany and France. In spite of repeated indications to
the contrary, France was still legally an occupied country.
Abetz received his instructions from Ribbentrop and
worked with the Vichy government. But he was disclaimed
by Hitler and Himmler whenever it suited their purposes.
The aged Marshal Pétain felt that he was being deceived
by all political quarters and often said as much when he
spoke with officers of the German Army.

The Todt Organization (the Labor Corps, or *Arbeitsdienst*) was also independent and obeyed so-called "Führer directives" issued by the Reich Minister for Arms and Munitions and the High Command. The Commander in Chief West could indicate his requirements to the Todt Organization, but he could not give it orders. The unbalanced strength of the coastal defenses and the Channel Islands is a striking example of this confusion.

Army Group B could not itself order construction of defensive installations along its thirteen-hundred-mile defense sector. It had to apply through these hopeless channels. It was useless to protest. The Todt Organization was overorganized and overmanned, so that it built very often just for the sake of building and urgent military requirements were neglected. Reichsminister Speer tried too late to remedy these evils.

During the retreat from France, high SS leaders and Luftwaffe commanders often withdrew their units into Germany, without regard to the situation at the moment, on the pretext that they needed to reorganize and bring their units up to strength. This gave their movements the appearance of a rout, which the hard-pressed fighting forces were attempting to avoid. Under such unfortunate conditions in the chain of command, it was often impossible to carry out the operational orders given at the last moment by Field Marshal von Rundstedt.

Field Marshal Rommel recalled his own experiences in Africa and the example of the Western Allies in the First and Second World Wars. The land, naval, and air forces of the United States and Great Britain for the invasion were all under the command of a Supreme Commander, General Eisenhower. Rommel demanded orally and in writing that all three services and the Todt Organization in his area be put under his command for one decisive defense effort.

Even after he had made repeated inquiries, his request was sharply refused. Hitler wanted to keep the command fluid; he did not want to give too much power to any one person, and particularly not to Rommel. Military requirements were sacrificed to Hitler's suspicions.

This concept of "divide and rule" broke the unity of the Western Command and delivered it to the forces of confusion.

ROMMEL AND HIS STAFF

The operational headquarters of Army Group B was located near the front in the Château La Roche Guyon. The Château stood on the western fringe of the fair Île de France in a great northward bend of the Seine and on its north bank. About forty miles downstream from Paris, between Mantes and Vernon, it was the seat of the Dukes de la Rochefoucauld. Built against the cliffs above the Seine, it had been a Norman stronghold in the year 1000, and the ruins of the old castle with its prominent tower still dominated the hill. Rommel permitted the ducal family to remain, and brought into the Château itself only the inner circle of his staff. The portrait of the most famous of the Dukes, the Marshal de la Rochefoucauld, hung in the hall of arms. It was he who had written the celebrated maxims—maxims which were being disregarded in our present situation. The philanthropist and politician, the Duke de la Rochefoucauld-Liancourt, was another eminent man who had been born in La Roche Guyon.

Field Marshal Rommel selected for himself a modest apartment on the ground floor, adjoining a rose terrace. The study was imbued with old French culture; and there were splendid tapestries and an inlaid Renaissance desk, on which Louvois had signed the revocation of the

Edict of Nantes in 1685. After the invasion of Normandy had begun and Allied air attacks increased, Rommel agreed with the Duke to store these art treasures in the family chapel under the cliff. There they remained undamaged.

The Headquarters of Army Group B consisted only of a small working staff, purposely kept small. There was the Chief of the General Staff, Lieutenant General Dr. Hans Speidel; the operations officer, Colonel von Tempelhoff; the intelligence officer (I C), Colonel Staubwasser; the adjutant, Colonel Freyberg (II A); and, as members of the special technical staff: Colonel General Lattman (Artillery); Lieutenant General Dr. Meise (Engineer Corps); Lieutenant General Gehrke (Signal Corps); and the naval adviser, Vice-Admiral Friedrich Ruge. There was also a General Staff officer of the Luftwaffe, adjutants, and war historians. The Quartermaster General's department, which had no executive authority, was abolished before the invasion, and its duties taken over by the Quartermaster General for France. Contrary to regulations, there was no National Socialist political officer in the Headquarters. This omission was one of the charges leveled at the Chief of Staff later on, when the Gestapo interrogated him. When Field Marshal Model took over command of the Army Group in August 1944, he immediately installed within the staff one of these secret police agents, who had the right to report directly to Himmler and Hitler's deputy, Martin Bormann.

In the work of the Army Group B Staff in the days of Marshal Rommel there was mutual agreement on military matters, and personal understanding. There was also outer and inner harmony and mental balance; the officers were free, in so far as possible, to use their own initiative. The working days of Marshal Rommel in the "quiet times" before the invasion were spent in purposeful work. He visited the troops almost daily without a large entourage, accompanied usually only by his adjutant, Captain Lang, and often by Vice-Admiral Ruge, to whom Rommel felt particularly close, because of his gallant and fine personality. The Marshal left his headquarters between five and six o'clock, after breakfasting with his Chief of Staff and discussing the most urgent business with him. He moved about his command until evening, making only a short pause for lunch with whatever unit he happened to be inspecting at the time. Conferences began soon after his return to La Roche Guyon and lasted until it was time for a simple supper, which was the same as the evening meal served to the whole staff.

The Marshal ate with the ten or twelve officers working most closely with him, and there were guests every day. He was frugal, drank little, and never smoked; he was open to any discussion that arose at the table.

After supper he took his customary stroll in the park of the Château, usually with General Speidel and Admiral Ruge. His favorite spot was beneath two mighty cedars, with a view of the peaceful valley of the Seine and the western sky. After further conferences, he went to bed early.

When he inspected the front, Rommel would explain the situation to the officers and men and tell of his own plans. He knew how to keep the right balance between praise and criticism. He placed great importance on the conduct of his troops towards the civil population and repeatedly reminded them of the laws of humanity in peace and war. He insisted that international conventions were to be kept to the letter, and he upheld a code of chivalry that had become strange in our day and age and was regarded by Hitler as a sign of weakness.

DISTRIBUTION OF THE GERMAN FORCES
IN THE SPRING OF 1944

a. *The Army:* The Commander in Chief of Army Group
B, Field Marshal Rommel, commanded two armies, with
eight army corps headquarters, twenty-four infantry divisions, and five Luftwaffe field division, which were units
composed of superfluous air force personnel. Field Marshal
Rommel's command included:

The Wehrmacht Commander for the Netherlands, who
had under his command one army corps headquarters
(LXXXVIII), two infantry divisions (347, 709) one Luftwaffe Field Division (16).

The Commander, Air General Christiansen, nicknamed
"Krischan," distinguished himself in the first World War
as captain of an auxiliary cruiser and was decorated with
the order Pour le Mérite. Then he became a pilot in the
Fleet Air Arm. He was recalled to service after 1933 as a
major general and appointed to high posts in the Luftwaffe.
He was a bluff, simple seaman and did not have the experience, education, and mental qualities to lead an army;
he knew very little of land warfare. This made his appointment as commander all the more unusual—there was no regard for military qualifications. Reichsmarshal Göring
merely wanted to place one of his own trusted men in a
key position. The Chief of Staff to Christiansen, Lieutenant
General von Wülisch, a General Staff and cavalry officer,
endeavored to offset the deficiencies of his chief, and was
given a free hand by Christiansen.

The Fifteenth Army consisted of four army corps headquarters (LXXXIX, LXXXII, LXVII, and LXXXI), six infantry divisions at the front (70—this division consisted of
soldiers with stomach ailments, but it fought well nevertheless—47, 49, 344, 348, 711); and two Luftwaffe field

divisions at the front (17 and 18); in the rear areas eight infantry divisions (64, 712, 182 Res., 326, 331, 85, 89, 346); and one Luftwaffe field division (19).

The Commander of the Fifteenth Army, Colonel General von Salmuth, was a man who had gained great tactical and operational experience in peace and in war. He had been Chief of Staff to Field Marshal von Bock in the western campaign of 1940, and in 1941 commanded the XXX Corps on the east front in the Crimea; during the critical winter, 1942–43, he led the Second Army at Kursk. He was relieved of that command after his steadfastness had been unjustifiably questioned. An enemy of the National Socialist system, he had discerned the coming catastrophe.

The Seventh Army consisted of three army corps headquarters (LXXXIV, LXXIV, LXX), and later the II Parachute Corps; seven infantry divisions at the front (716, 352, 243—not full strength—319—on the Channel Islands—266, 343, and 265). In the rear areas there were two infantry divisions (84 and 353), the 91st Airborne Division, and later two parachute divisions.

The Seventh Army Commander, Colonel General Dollmann, was an artillery officer. He was thoroughly schooled in General Staff work and in the command of troops, but his only practical experience was the crossing of the upper Rhine in the western campaign of 1940, not in itself a decisive operation. His health was not good.

The methods of Hitler had wounded him deeply both as a soldier and as a man. He died of a heart attack in his battle headquarters on June 29, 1944, a few days after Hitler had demanded his dismissal, which Rommel had refused.

As for *Panzer units*, there was a General of Armored Forces in the west, stationed within the Army Group area, with a corps command (I SS Panzer Corps) and five Panzer divisions (1 SS, 12 SS, 2, 21, and 116).

South of the Loire there was the LXIII Panzer Corps with the 9th and 11th Panzer divisions; and the 2nd and 17th SS Panzer divisions. Some of these formations were made up of fresh troops; others were in the process of being reorganized and brought up to strength.

The general commanding Panzer troops in the west, General Baron Geyr von Schweppenburg, was stationed in Paris with a training staff, which was later to become a tactical command staff. In matters of organization and training he was responsible to the Inspector General of Armored Forces, Colonel General Guderian. In operational matters he was immediately subordinate to the Commander in Chief for the West. Schweppenburg was an unusual personality, capable in both military and political fields and able to make deductions from experiences gathered in the conduct of modern warfare. He had been unswerving and fearless as military attaché in London, in reporting the increasing isolation of Germany, and these warnings led to his recall.

The entire Atlantic front of 2,500 miles was manned by some sixty semimobile infantry divisions. They were composed of men of the older age groups. Battle-tried men were scarce. Both the officers and noncommissioned officers were, for the most part, overage, and unequal to the task that was to fall to their lot. They were poorly equipped and could be compared with the type of infantry division found at the end of the first World War. The number of horses available for transport was so inadequate as to leave them practically immobile and hardly able to obtain provisions. They were by no means a match for the motorized and mobile enemy that we expected, if the invasion should develop into mobile warfare. Field Marshal Rommel had repeatedly brought these deficiencies to the notice of the High Command and did not hesitate to reveal to Hitler personally the fact that these divisions were useless for modern warfare. His views were rejected, and Hitler referred him to his war directive, according to which the soldier's duty was "to stand and be killed in his defenses" but not to be "mobile."

The armored divisions had not been brought to full strength, and their training was unfinished. They were short of tried officers and of matériel. But the fighting potential of the armored divisions was higher than that of the stationary infantry divisions, although it was only about thirty per cent of the 1940 and 1941 standards of such divisions. The joint training operations with the Luftwaffe were repeatedly sought without success. The enemy, on the other hand, had developed air-ground co-operation to a remarkable degree.

The chiefs of the German Luftwaffe showed little understanding of these requirements. There was no unified command of the armed forces in the field, and so it was impossible to have combined exercises of the Army and the Luftwaffe, even in the field of radio communications.

b. *The German Navy:* The German Navy was in a tragic dilemma throughout the war. Its strength was never adequate to carry out its missions. Indeed, it was so weak and its strategic position so unfavorable that it could only be an auxiliary service. As the war spread, its tasks multiplied beyond those in continental waters that Hitler had first laid down. After Grand Admiral Raeder, who had kept free of politics, had been dismissed, there was no expert naval opinion to counterbalance the ideas of Hitler. The Navy had generally been more subservient than the Army to the dictator's policy. The acquiescence of the Navy to

Hitler's political policies was confirmed when Grand Admiral Dönitz was appointed to succeed Raeder against Raeder's wishes and recommendations.

The overestimation of the importance of the Navy which had become prevalent after Marshal von Blomberg left the scene in 1938 had its roots in the lack of a true co-ordinating organ in the defense forces—one that could define missions clearly to the three services. This lack of insight into the problem of co-ordination for total warfare was to have dangerous results. The Navy, like the Luftwaffe, went its own way and did not always realize the necessity for a unified command of the armed forces. Later it became more closely connected with the Party and was vigilant in defending its own prerogatives, although the naval officers at land stations achieved practical and comradely co-operation with the army.

The naval commander in the west, Admiral Krancke (Chief of Staff, Vice-Admiral Hoffmann), probably on instructions from Dönitz, insisted on his independence, and when disaster was impending could not see his way clear to give unstinted help to the army. Admiral Krancke held his special Marine Security units, of some 5,000 men, in Paris, instead of making them available for the desperate battle at the front. He only offered to use them on the evening of July 20, 1944, to free the security units which had been arrested in France by order of the military governor. Thus the Navy was used against the Army.

The German Navy in the west consisted of several destroyers, ten to fifteen torpedo boats, a few motor torpedo flotillas, a number of mine-sweepers, patrol boats, tankers and repair ships. In case of invasion, forty U-boats were to have put to sea from the Atlantic coast. Only six of them weighed anchor, and these could achieve no success in the face of the overwhelming Allied sea and air superiority.

The effectiveness of the U-boats was no longer worth while in relation to the losses they sustained.

For a long time there had been no German sea and air reconnaissance off the coast.

On the evening of June 14, 1944, thirty-eight surface vessels were destroyed, including four torpedo boats, during an Allied air attack on the pier and submarine pens of Le Havre. Nearly all the torpedo boats and patrol boats were put out of action. The enemy squadrons came in at a low altitude and carried out their destruction unmolested.

The German Navy in western waters had by June 29, according to information furnished by Dönitz in Berchtesgaden, no more than one torpedo boat, twelve patrol boats and eight U-boats with Schnorkel equipment—a new safety device to prevent U-boats from being detected by enemy radar. The large number of shore installations in France—a number which corresponded neither to the size of the German Navy nor to its sea mission—still further confused the already muddled command situation. An example of this confusion was the coastal artillery fire-control system. The Navy claimed the responsibility for coastal gunnery as long as the invader was sea-borne, but after a landing was made the Army should take over the entire coastal artillery. This led to a disagreement in the planning stages between the tactical artillery principles of the Navy and of the Army, particularly in such matters as the placing of guns and observation posts as well as the actual servicing of the guns.

Army Group B tried repeatedly, but without success, to annul this order, but Hitler rejected Rommel's demands. The Naval Command in the west was mistaken in its estimate of the inland range of Allied naval guns. It did not believe that they could reach more than ten miles inland on steep coasts and thirteen on flat coasts. Actually, the Allied warships fired on targets twenty-five miles inland, as the troops defending Caen were to discover.

c. *The Luftwaffe:* The question as to the best use to be made of the German Air Forces on the western front, as in the Reich, was a burning problem. It was not possible for the Army to obtain precise information from the Air Staff as to Luftwaffe strength, duties, and possible employment. Reichsmarshal Göring avoided discussion of this subject or gave ambiguous answers. He sought no first hand information in these decisive months, attempting instead to direct the air forces from Karinhall or East Prussia. There could be no discussion with Göring about air warfare, since he did not seem to be sufficiently informed about his own branch of the service.

The Third Air Fleet in the west was under the direct command of Göring through its Commander in Chief, Marshal Sperrle. The latter's Chief of Staff was Lieutenant General Koller and later Major General Plocher. The High Command of the Armed Forces had only a limited right to indicate the missions it wished to have performed.

The officer commanding the Third Air Fleet, Sperrle, was a man of unusual vitality; but the more clearly he saw the unholy disorder in Hitler's leadership, the more he expended his energies in bitter sarcasm. He tried to work with us in a comradely manner whenever he could, especially since he shared the political views of Rommel. Sperrle was made the scapegoat for the shortcomings of Göring and dismissed by Hitler on August 18.

Responsible reports from the Third Air Fleet indicated that at the beginning of June it had only ninety bombers and seventy fighters in operational condition out of a total of 500 aircraft in the west. These few could not be put into action, so great was the Allied air supremacy. The "first batch" of 1,000 jet fighters promised by Hitler on April 1, 1944, to the Chief of Staff of Army Group B failed to materialize.

The enemy air force supported landing operations on June 6 with 25,000 sorties.

The air forces of Great Britain and the United States had ruled the sky since the spring of 1944 and paralyzed all German air activities. Satisfactory reconnaissance could no longer be achieved. Our photographs of British territory could not be made, let alone photographs of British harbor installations and the coastal waters adjacent to the ports. It was no longer even possible to concentrate enough fighter strength to oppose the relentless enemy bombing squadrons. German defensive air concentrations to halt Allied sorties could not be effected, as the Luftwaffe was scattered all over the west, with no real strength anywhere. The well-manned and highly developed fighter bombers of the Allies halted all daylight movement and inflicted heavy losses. Bomber squadrons destroyed railway junctions and crossroads, as well as buildings, so thoroughly that the supply difficulties in case of invasion seemed likely to be insurmountable. Destruction of railways west of a line drawn between Brussels, Paris, and Orléans made it impossible for us to organize a regular supply and replacement system by rail after the middle of May. There was neither sufficient motor transport capacity nor gasoline to take over the supply burden from the railroads.

It was the supply problem that was one of the reasons for our defeat in the African campaign of 1942, the Russian operations of 1942, and the mobile fighting in the west in 1944. All the Seine bridges below Paris and all the Loire bridges below Orléans were destroyed by bombing before June 6, 1944. Underwater bridges (tunnels under the rivers) had not been built, although they were suggested on more than one occasion. There was not enough bridge-building equipment to make temporary spans.

The enemy air forces steadily increased their attacks on the occupied territories and on the Reich itself.

It is deserving of mention that in spite of the overwhelming superiority of the Allied air forces, the few German pilots took to the air without any hope of success wherever the enemy had left airfields intact.

Field Marshal Rommel did not fail to emphasize to Hitler, both in written reports and in conversation, before the beginning of the invasion, the importance of having all three services fight side by side. He emphasized that the inferiority of the Luftwaffe was apt to be a decisive factor. He compared this situation with the experiences in Africa and the consequent supply problems. "It ought to be dawning on the High Command in this fifth year of war," he told Hitler, "that the air force in co-operation with the army will be not only decisive in battle, but will decide the war." There was a hollow echo to all such warnings. They were brushed off with promises of new "miracle weapons" and thousands of jet fighters.

But Rommel was not satisfied by vague references to "miracle weapons" and made personal inquiries to Reichsminister Speer as to how these inventions and new developments were progressing and when they might be put to use. He was told that between the scientific development of the atom bomb and its production, much time would elapse. Professor Otto Hahn had worked out the scientific process, but Germany lacked the mighty industrial power for its production that the United States commanded. In the spring of 1943, when Germany was just about to begin production, the hydroelectric plant in Norway was destroyed by British and Norwegian demolition troops and, after being repaired by October 1943, was completely destroyed by bombing. Professor Werner Heisenberg of the University of Göttingen said: "We have often been asked by the British and Americans why we did not try to produce the atom bomb in Germany. The simplest answer that can be given to this question is that we could not succeed in this undertaking during the war."

In this connection we must also point to our lack of air supremacy. U.S. Air Force experiences with dropping the first atom bomb in August 1945 demonstrated that strong air forces are necessary to carry the atom bomb safely to its target.

Rommel complained more than once of the overstaffing of the Luftwaffe in the western command, where it maintained an excessively large and independent system of communications requiring 50,000 men. The ground services of the Luftwaffe in the west consisted of more than 300,000 men—a ratio of one hundred men on the ground for every one in the air, while in other air corps it was usually ten to one. This proportion could only be ascribed to the ambition of Göring and of Himmler to create a private army—a peculiar tendency that is common to all revolutionary leaders.

The III Flak Corps, in defiance of all common sense and the demands of Army Group B, was put under the command of the Third Air Fleet in Paris and thus of Göring in East Prussia. In consequence, it was badly placed when invasion came and could not be moved quickly enough. Its concentrated firepower would have been of considerable importance in the first days of landing. This excellent weapon was never used under unified fire control in decisive sectors of the battlefield. The commanding officer of the III Flak Corps was ordered away by Göring during the battle of Normandy without the knowledge of Army Group B and remained absent for days.

The air war was an intensified version of the disaster that had already taken place in Africa and Italy. The enemy ruled the air over the battlefield, over the occupied countries, and even over the Reich itself. The German pilots had vanished from the sky.

Because of mistakes in planning, organization, and leadership, the Luftwaffe had been worn down and demoralized before the final battles took place. Germany failed in all attempts to carry out independent air operations—the air battle over Britain after the mass of the British army had escaped from Dunkirk in 1940, the "extinction" of the British Navy, the battle of the Atlantic, the defense of Germany from British-American attacks, the attempt to supply Stalingrad, Cherkassy, the Crimea, and Africa by air—all these were sad chapters in a historical sequence of failures. The courageous German airmen were the victims of their leaders.

The British and American air forces, in contrast, effectively speeded up the outcome of the war both on the western front and against Germany.

THE ATLANTIC WALL

The Atlantic Wall was a fortified coastal line of uneven strength. It had been well fortified at points where the German High Command suspected the Allies would make landings: along the Channel—especially at Cap Gris Nez—at the mouth of the Seine, the northern shoulder of the Cotentin peninsula, the Channel Islands, Brest, and Lorient. But the coast of Calvados, and particularly the sector between the coast and Bayeux, was practically unfortified when Marshal Rommel took over command.

Hitler had decided in 1941 that the main line of resistance was to be the beaches. But the length of this front permitted only a system of strong points. A continuous line of fortifications was out of the question. The Channel coast and the Channel Islands of Guernsey, Jersey, and Sark, opposite St. Mâlo, were to be made "mightiest fortresses," in accordance with an eight-year plan. This was the will of Hitler. Therefore, an "offensive battery group" was set up at Cap Gris Nez: the Lindemann battery (three guns of 40.6 cm. caliber), the "Grosser Kurfürst" (Great Elector) battery (four 28 cm. guns), the Todt battery (four 38 cm. guns), and the "Friedrich August" battery (three 30.3 guns). This was the backbone of the Channel defenses.

On the small Channel Islands, early in February 1944, there were in readiness eleven heavy batteries with thirty-eight guns, while the whole coast of the mainland between Dieppe and St. Nazaire, a distance of six hundred miles, had the same number of batteries with thirty-seven guns in all. A division strengthened with armored and antiaircraft regiments was provided as garrison for these islands, but no airfields were built, although these islands could only have had importance as bases for launching aircraft. Rommel bitterly opposed the strengthening of the Channel Island defenses and demanded that its useless garrison be withdrawn.

The whole defensive system suffered from the lack of any over-all plan, from a lack of matériel, and above all from a lack of authority, which resulted from the confused chain of command.

In 1944 the coastal defenses consisted only of strong points with radar stations, command posts, and battery placements. The redoubts and dugouts were constructed as field rather than as permanent fortifications, and were seldom reinforced by concrete, because of a lack of material. These strong points were often miles apart.

The Naval Command had declared that the Vire-Orne

sector of the coast was not likely to be invaded, because of
its dangerous reefs. There were only one and a half divisions
of troops on this thirty-mile stretch of coast.

Rommel was disappointed with these fortifications when
he made his first complete inspection of the Atlantic Wall
during the winter of 1943–44, and tried to make up for
the omissions by setting his troops to work constructing
defenses, particularly on the Normandy coast. He worked
out new means of obstructing enemy landings.

The entire development of the coastal defense, the design and construction of the fortifications, had been entrusted to an engineer of the Todt Organization, who had
neither tactical nor strategical training, no over-all view of
the total war situation, and no experience in dealing with
the armed forces.

Between 1941 and 1943, the Army, Navy and Todt
Organization were not able to agree on a unified plan of
coastal defenses, especially artillery placements, since their
basic principles were in conflict. Rommel brought about a
radical change in the approach to this question. He showed
not only a high degree of personal interest but also extraordinary technical knowledge, which disconcerted the spe-
cialists. His orders contained his own sketches embodying
new designs and suggestions which were adopted.

To make an enemy landing more difficult, underwater
obstacles were laid in the form of artificial coral reefs. The
shallow water approaches to beaches were to be mined and
harbors were to be made unusable.

The high-water mark along the beaches was mined as
a continuous main line of defense. Artillery firepower—
there was only one battery to every fourteen miles or so
—could not be greatly increased, mainly because fire-control instruments were lacking.

In this connection the Marshal sought to improvise

weapons and methods of fire which would fill the gap caused by the lack of a mass of artillery. He accepted the idea put forward by the 21st Panzer Division to use salvo guns, known as "Stalin organs," which would face the sea. But it was too late to give effect to this idea.

Aware of the increasing danger of concentrated air attacks, he dispersed the troop billets as a safety measure. A "land front" was organized to cope with airborne troop landings by sealing off a coastal defense zone from two to three miles in depth, depending on the terrain. Thus it was hoped to prevent airborne troops landing in the interior from joining with a coastal invasion force. As a defensive measure against parachute troops and gliders, the Marshal had tree trunks rammed into open fields, connected with barbed wire, and often mined. This time- and material-consuming work was confined to the most vulnerable spots.

Rommel had gained a clear conception of airborne landing operations even in unfavorable weather, and trained his troops accordingly. He requested the Navy to lay mines in the sea approaches, but the first mine-laying operations took place in the mouth of the Gironde, instead of the Seine.

The type of mine that it was proposed to use against invading forces would have to be laid immediately before an attack. This was not done before the invasion on the Normandy coast. The High Command had turned down proposals to use aircraft in laying offensive mines.

Most of this defense work had to be done with local labor. Rommel gave orders that, as a matter of principle, no French citizen could be forced to work, but that volunteers would be well paid. The French laborers were to be treated exactly the same as the Germans. He told the inhabitants that it was to their advantage to co-operate in the construction of obstacles, since these would lessen the chance of airborne landings and, thereby, the inclusion of their area in the battle zone.

Flooding was limited by the terrain to the Le Havre area, the Dives valley, and the east coast of the Cotentin peninsula. There it was possible to construct fresh-water reservoirs, and preparations were being made. Rommel directed that flooding by sea water, which had inflicted damage lasting ten years after the first World War, was to be avoided under all circumstances.

Propaganda for the Atlantic Wall began in 1942, when turning back the British and Canadian reconnaissance force at Dieppe was represented as "a tremendous defensive success." The Royal Navy, the Army, and the R.A.F. had carried out a large-scale commando attack on both sides of Dieppe. As a reconnaissance in force, it was designed to keep German forces tied down and collect experience in combined landing operations. Captured British orders showed clearly that this was a limited objective operation with respect to the time factor, the forces involved and the ground to be captured. German propaganda claimed a big success for the defense, to distract public attention from reverses on the Russian front. The High Command in the west regrettably associated itself with these exaggerated claims.

As early as the summer of 1938, during the construction of the Westwall, Goebbels had acquired experience in exploiting fortifications for propaganda purposes. In order to conceal its inadequacies and to deceive the enemy, he now launched a wave of propaganda regarding the Atlantic Wall. He used as his example the heavy "offensive battery group" at Cap Gris Nez, and made it appear that the entire Atlantic Wall was of equal strength.

Marshal Rommel, in order to gain time for his political

intentions, which will be discussed later, permitted his new defense measures against air landings and on the beaches to be made public in an exaggerated form. For the same reason he allowed himself to figure prominently in films and in the news. But when he heard of Dr. Goebbels' directive that the press was not to mention the Allied superiority in the air, he protested against this deception of the public, which would surely shake the confidence of the German people in its leaders.

The following deceptive operations were practiced by the military. Rumors were spread about the arrival of fictitious troops and reinforcements. Dummy headquarters and "advance personnel" were moved about. Movements by rail were worked out for nonexistent reinforcements, and orders went through the entire chain of command, including the French railway officials with their complicated paper work. Columns of trucks were moving about day and night, and dummy installations were being constructed.

Rommel had no illusions about the effectiveness of these stratagems, but he was ready to try anything to gain time. It was impossible to control the effects of these propaganda efforts because of the arbitrary and uninhibited methods of Goebbels.

Rommel later asked Hitler to stop the fictitious Atlantic Wall propaganda, in which he himself had been obliged to figure.

STAFF STUDIES BEFORE THE INVASION

At Berchtesgaden on April 1, 1944, before entering on his new duties with the Army Group, Rommel's new chief of staff, General Speidel, had asked for instructions on strategy. Hitler and the High Command declared that any such directive was "superfluous." The Commander in Chief in the West and Army Group B had strict orders that the

coast was to be rigidly defended; there was to be no freedom for strategic operations. In case of a local landing, the
enemy was to be driven from the beaches back into the
sea. The lessons of Salerno and Nettuno were not taken
into account. At both invasions on the west coast of Italy,
the British had succeeded in landing a superior force with
naval and air support and made good their footholds. German Panzer reserves could not be effectively brought into
action because of the distance involved and enemy superiority in the air.

The Chief of Staff was told that when invasion threatened, some eight to ten full strength Panzer divisions would
be brought up in time, together with new jet fighters and
naval units, particularly U-boats. Annihilating use would
be made of the "reprisal weapon" (the V–1 and V–2
rockets).

Hitler's decision to hold the coast line at any price was
rooted in his desire for prestige, as was the case at Stalingrad, in the Don battles, in the Crimea, in Sicily and in
Italy. But "he who would defend all, defends nothing,"
because "defense lines cover more ground than available
troops can defend . . ." said Frederick the Great. "Little
minds want to defend everything; sensible men concentrate on the essentials." Germany's advantage of maneuver-
ability was abandoned in favor of rigid coastal defenses.
This factor reduced the risks inherent in a large-scale
Allied landing; the British and Americans ruled the sea;
there was no German fleet capable of giving battle. The
German air force had been put out of action, eliminating
a critical threat to the Allied invasion. In its manning and
armaments the Atlantic Wall was no more than a thin line,
without depth or substantial reserves. The Allied land
forces were far superior, not only in numbers and equipment, but also in mobility.

There were no historical precedents of landing operations on this scale with which comparison was possible. In the Egyptian campaign of 1798, Napoleon had to reckon with the superior navy of his enemy, which destroyed his own fleet at Aboukir Bay. There was a strong Russian navy in 1854, but, surprisingly, it was kept inactive when the Allies embarked for the Crimea. The Russians also had a strong fleet in 1904. But the Japanese, before being able to land in the Bay of Korea, had to destroy this fleet, and made a surprise attack on Port Arthur similar to the Pearl Harbor attack of 1941. The closest historical parallel to the German naval position in 1944 is that of the Southern States during the American Civil War. The Northern States possessed a superior navy to which the Southern States could offer little opposition.

Field Marshal Rommel, mindful of the recent experiences in Italy, was certain that the Allies would quickly surmount the classic crisis that comes in the first three days of a landing while the beachhead is being consolidated, unless the relative strength of the defense to the attack could be drastically altered, especially at sea and in the air. He initiated staff studies on probable Allied intentions after a successful landing, and how they were to be countered without, for the time being, deviating from Hitler's orders for a rigid defense of the coast. He assumed that, as Hitler had promised, an adequate Panzer reserve would be available in the region of Paris.

The staff therefore worked out the following possibilties in case of enemy landings:

Between the Seine and the Loire. Counter-operation: withdrawal to the Seine line, which was to be held; attack south of the Seine from the east and the south to wipe out the forces which had landed.

Between the Somme and the Seine. Counter-operation:

3. German Tanks Moving to the Normandy Front

4. Invading American Forces on the French Channel Coast

retreat to and hold strong points on the Amiens-Vernon line and on the Oise; counterattack between the rivers, although this would lead to difficult frontal engagements.

North of the Somme (unlikely because of the terrain, and for strategic and tactical considerations). Counteroperation: attack from the south northwards.

South of the Loire and on the Mediterranean coast. Abandon southern France and defend the Loire line. Muster a strategic reserve of two to three armies and as many Panzer units as possible between the bend of the Loire and Jura mountains for mobile operations.

South of the Seine and on the Mediterranean coast simultaneously. Abandon southern France, defend the Seine-Yonne-Canal de Bourgogne line. Muster a strategic reserve in the Troyes-Dijon-Langres-St. Dizier area.

Many variations of these possibilities were studied, but it was assumed in all cases that German Panzer units would be combined with sufficient air forces. In addition, all other possibilities were weighed and planned for—evacuation of France, Belgium, and Holland, as well as a retreat behind the Meuse and then the Westwall. These operations were planned for either under battle conditions or after an armistice. In both cases, the technical, strategical, and time factors were taken into account.

Had Hitler decided upon strategic operations after the invasion had succeeded—such as, perhaps, a timely withdrawal from southern France, a holding operation on the Seine line, or formation of a strategic reserve for a counteroffensive—the catastrophic events of the summer of 1944 would not have developed so rapidly. Rommel explained these ideas to Hitler on June 17 and on June 29, 1944, with the result that on July 2 the Führer issued a stern order reminiscent of the Stalingrad winter campaign: "Every enemy attempt to break through is to be prevented by tenaciously holding our ground. It is forbidden to shorten the front. It is not permitted to maneuver freely."

As the Battle of Normandy reached its critical stage, Rommel decided to resort to a war of movement against Hitler's express will. He took this decision late, but not too late, for it preceded the decisive breakthrough at Avranches. He was not destined to carry through this redeeming decision.

THE PROBLEM OF STRATEGIC RESERVES

The strategical principle governing the conduct of German operations on the western front was to be a rigid defense of the coast at all costs. A single Panzer corps of six divisions was available as a mobile strategic reserve.

The Commander in Chief for the West, Field Marshal von Rundstedt, thought along the strategic lines of the old school without taking into account the lessons of the Russian war and the Mediterranean campaigns, and without evaluating the battle tactics of the British and Americans. He proposed to hold this small reserve south and east of Paris, from where it would be brought up after an enemy landing. He thought that he could thus retain freedom of action and make full use of the former German superiority in open warfare. This strategy would have been correct, had the German naval and air forces been equal, or nearly equal, in strength to those of the enemy.

Because of our weaker forces and the vulnerable condition of our defenses at the coast, time would be required to prepare and execute such an operation. The coastal defenses were too inadequate to give us the delay in time that was necessary. The cornerstone of the operation would collapse long before reserves could be brought up.

Rommel wanted to bring up the six Panzer divisions that were available and place them close to the area where in-

vasion was expected. He remembered the lessons learned
from the landings in Italy. Large-scale local landings could
not be repulsed without these Panzer reserves. One or two
Panzer divisions would be no better than a "fire brigade,"
considering the lack of transport facilities and the Allied
air supremacy. Rommel considered that at least five Panzer
divisions would be necessary to carry out his mission.
These Panzer divisions would be prepared for all eventual-
ities—counterattack, defense against mass airborne landings, lateral movements from one front to another, including crossings of the Seine, and rear-guard actions.
Wherever they were stationed, they should also help in
the work of deepening the defenses and erecting obstacles
against gliders and parachutists.

As a minimum, five or six Panzer divisions within the
Army Group command would be required for these various tasks, and even so it would be difficult for immobile
coastal defense forces without air or naval support to operate against a fully motorized enemy with crushing sea
and air superiority.

The success of the enemy air offensive since April 1944
made it possible to predict that, if the reserves were held
so far back—in the Paris area for example—they would certainly arrive too late.

"If we cannot get at the enemy immediately after he
lands," declared Rommel at a conference, "we will never
be able to make another move, because of his vastly superior air forces. . . . If we are not able to repulse the enemy
at sea or throw him off the mainland in the first forty-eight
hours, then the invasion will have succeeded, and the war
will be lost for lack of a strategic reserve and the complete
absence of our navy and Luftwaffe."

The lessons of Nettuno and Salerno were full of significance for us. All the experiences of this war had taught

us that only divisions directly responsible to the group commander and actually located in the battle area could really be employed at the decisive moment. Decisions to use the so-called High Command reserves usually came too late. And when they were thrown into battle they were employed in an improvised and amateurish fashion, because of "intuitive" orders from the Führer, and were, therefore, sacrificed. For political reasons also, the Marshal thought it appropriate to have reliable Panzer units close at hand for any eventuality.

It was especially difficult for Rommel to carry out a static defense when in his mind he worked out plans for mobile warfare. In Africa, after all, he had given impressive evidence of his ability to wage a mobile war with modern Panzer units. But he saw clearly that such operations would be impossible if the flank was penetrated in the vital areas north or south of the Seine.

Rommel repeatedly requested that strategic reserves of some six to eight armored and five to seven motorized divisions be made available and stationed east of Paris under the unified command of the Western Panzer Group, as Hitler had promised the Chief of Staff of Army Group B on April 1, 1944. According to the staff studies, this would be the group to begin mobile operations against the Allies after a successful landing and to maintain freedom of action.

Rommel also proposed that defense lines should be located and built in the interior of France, in accord with these strategic concepts of his, and thought first of a Seine-Yonne line of defense.

Field Marshal von Rundstedt approved the views and requests of Rommel after they had examined all aspects of each other's strategical and tactical ideas. He agreed that the Panzer forces which were immediately available should be brought up and stationed close to the most threatened coastal sectors north and south of the Seine.

The Inspector General of Panzer Forces, Colonel General Guderian, who had adhered to the von Rundstedt strategy, as did also General Geyr von Schweppenburg, visited the Army Group Headquarters in May 1944, listened to Rommel's views and the battle directives issued for the west, and raised no strenuous objection to Rommel's intention to bring up the available Panzer divisions. He also intended to demand of Hitler that a strong armored operational group be brought up immediately. All promises of the High Command were broken, and no mobile or armored reserves of any kind were brought up to the western front in time.

These promises of Hitler gave evidence of his frivolous mentality. No additional forces could be released from the east unless Hitler could decide to shorten the eastern front drastically. At the Führer's headquarters, decisions were made on tactical rather than strategic principles.

Events proved Rommel to be right. The enemy air supremacy and the flexible conduct of his air forces made it impossible to bring Panzer divisions from the interior of France to the coast in time, and impossible to put them into action as a unit. The Panzer divisions were broken up before they could reach the Normandy front.

Had there been more Panzer forces close to the front, and could they have been used in the first three critical days after the initial landing, the circumstances would have been considerably different.

iii

ROMMEL'S POLITICAL DEDUCTIONS AND PREPARATIONS

O N THE EVENING of April 15, 1944, Rommel's new Chief of Staff reported on the situation at the eastern front and on the impressions he gained at the Führer's headquarters. Rommel explained his own thoughts regarding the conduct of the war and politics in general. The Field Marshal summed up:

The Crimea was lost, the eastern front had been drawn back into eastern Rumania. The Russian war potential had been greatly increased by British and American deliveries under the Lend-Lease Act. Decisive Russian operations were to be expected during the summer. Hitler had issued Basic Order No. 1, dated January 13, 1940, forbidding his Commanders in Chief to draw up any kind of situation reports. Using neutral sources, particularly the Swiss newspapers and foreign broadcasts, the Army Group learned something of the outcome of Allied political discussions and of their probable applications.

Rommel's tactical experience was based on the raid carried out by his 7th Panzer ("Phantom") Division in 1940, and the campaigns in North Africa. In May and

June 1940, Division Commander Rommel had crossed the
Meuse near Dinant, had broken through the Belgian-French
fortifications, and was the first German general to reach
the Channel and, later, the Atlantic coast. He stabilized the
situation in North Africa in 1941 with weak German
forces, and then was able to launch a successful attack. He
had no personal experience on the Russian front, but took
pains to collect information and to utilize the lessons
learned in Russia. His thoughts kept returning to the events
of the summer of 1942. The small German-Italian African
army then stood only sixty miles from Alexandria and
Cairo after the sudden capture of Tobruk, ready to push
on to the Suez Canal and the Nile, and to cut a main artery
of the British Empire. The Marshal had demanded adequate Italian naval and air support to maintain his supply
lines and bolster the momentum of the attack, which had
decreased to an alarming degree the further it advanced.
This support was not forthcoming. By their inactivity the
Italian navy and air force unconsciously helped the Allies.
Hitler had said, "I believe Mussolini more than my German generals," whereupon Rommel challenged him to visit
the front and see for himself. Hitler refused to go to the
front; he had not visited any front since 1941.

Montgomery's vastly superior armored forces began
their counteroffensive from well-supplied and secure bases,
supported by air forces that were overwhelming for those
days. The Royal Navy and the Royal Air Force blocked
all Rommel's supplies. Conscious of his responsibility, Rommel demanded permission to retreat from El Alamein.
Hitler radioed an emotional order: "Forward to Cairo!
Conquer or die!"

Rommel, quite unmoved by this, ordered a retreat to
save his troops from destruction. He had been given too
many assignments for "world conquest" without being

given the means necessary to carry them out. Rommel retained two deep impressions from the African campaign: a high respect for the world power of Britain and a low esteem for the Italian ally. The British and Dominion troops appeared to him to be first-class in leadership, morale, and efficiency, and their matériel, in quantity and quality, superior to the German. He had just as high an opinion of the American forces.

Rommel had repeatedly warned orally and in writing against relying on the Italians. His objections were based not only on the Italian military and foreign policy, which had finally dragged Germany into the Balkan adventure, but also on an exact knowledge of the political, military, mental, and economic structure of Italy.

His views brought him into conflict with Adolf Hitler and the High Command, who, believing it to be to their interest, had ordered that the British be ridiculed and the Italians extolled on every possible occasion. This clash of opinion sharpened during the winter of 1942–43, when Rommel proposed that the African front be abandoned and the troops transferred to the Russian front. He wanted to sacrifice an unimportant theater of war in order to reinforce a decisive effort.

By force of circumstance, Rommel had become acquainted with the French problem while still in Africa. The German High Command and the Foreign Office had negotiated with Admiral Darlan and General Huntziger in the winter of 1940–41, and in the course of 1941, for the purpose of protecting the rear of the German Afrika Korps. The immoderation of Hitler, who made demands that the French government could not possibly have accepted, caused these negotiations to collapse. A foresighted German statesman, disregarding Mussolini's claims, would, by 1940, have reached an agreement with France to include

Morocco, Algeria, and Tunisia in a European-African defense system. A few days after El Alamein, United States forces landed in French North Africa, French resistance ceased, and the Afrika Korps felt the consequences.

Erwin Rommel's stay in France gave him the opportunity to study the land and the people. He loved the French countryside and had deep sympathy for the sorely tried French people. He thought it intolerable to maintain the status of an armistice for four years and by this means systematically to discredit at home and abroad the regime of Marshal Pétain.

He believed in the mission of France, and therefore felt that it was essential to work out a Franco-German peace which would bring reconciliation, and he believed that the French should no longer be treated as enemies. At the conference with Hitler at Margival on the afternoon of June 17, he expressed his misgivings concerning the official German policy towards France and warned the Führer against rule by the Secret Police of the SS and the Sauckel program.

Rommel saw the military situation on April 15 as follows. Invasion in the west was a certainty, and defense with the forces available could not be assured. Later in the year a general offensive of the Red Army could be expected; in Italy the Allies were advancing slowly but steadily northward and wearing down the German forces. On the basis of his knowledge of the Italian terrain and the battle conditions, Rommel recommended abandoning central and southern Italy and withdrawing to a Pisa-Florence-Ravenna line. The High Command rejected his suggestions and told him to concern himself with his own theater of war. The defenses of the vulnerable coasts of Italy were scattered and weak, and were an open invitation to the enemy.

The political situation was even more hopeless than the military. Germany stood alone; Italy had become an enemy, since the sham dictatorship of Mussolini in northern Italy was meaningless in the rest of the country.

From Finland, Bulgaria, and Rumania came unintelligible and conflicting reports regarding the governments and peoples. No serious attempt was made to come to an understanding with one enemy in order to isolate the other. The foreign policy of Germany was as rigid and unimaginative as its military strategy.

One of the subjects of the first conference with the Field Marshal was the ideas of Dr. Goerdeler, the former Lord Mayor of Leipzig. These ideas had been conveyed to the Chief of Staff, for transmission to Rommel, during conversations at Freudenstadt (in Württemberg) on April 14 with Dr. Strölin, Lord Mayor of Stuttgart. Goerdeler had requested Strölin, at the end of 1943, to get in touch with Rommel and convince him that Hitler and his regime must be eliminated if Germany and Europe were to be saved. The mayor of Stuttgart, whom the Field Marshal had long repected as an active and intelligent man, referred on this occasion to his first conversation with Rommel, in February 1944. In that conversation the possibilities of a legal change of government and the means of ending the war had been discussed. Reports from the military, in particular from the former Chief of the General Staff, General Beck, and from the Quartermaster General, Artillery General Wagner, supplemented this political estimate. All agreed that a way must be found without delay to end the war before the inevitable catastrophe destroyed all possibility of negotiating a settlement. Rommel and his Chief of Staff discovered that their own political views were identical. In his typically forceful manner, the Field Marshal condemned the excesses of Hitler in human and military matters and in affairs of state, his disdain for European unity, and lack of feeling for humanity.

There followed a series of important preparatory discussions.

The Military Governor of Belgium and Northern France was Infantry General Alexander von Falkenhausen. Awarded the Pour le Mérite in the first World War, his intellectual and human qualities made him one of the most influential personalities not only in the west but in the entire Germany Army. Rommel had served under him when von Falkenhausen was Commandant of the Infantry School in Dresden, and revered this truly perspicacious person. Before the first World War he was military attaché in Japan, and had become military adviser to Marshal Chiang Kai-Shek in 1934, succeeding Generals von Seeckt and Wetzell. He knew the British and Americans as well as he did the peoples of the Far East. He had attained a rare detachment, and often quoted the observation of Confucius that power corrupts men, and absolute power is their undoing. In the face of incredible difficulties, he succeeded in counteracting Hitler's orders in Belgium and Northern France and governed this area as a gentleman. Belgium's recovery after the war is evidence of his good administration. Von Falkenhausen was replaced by Gauleiter Grohé on July 15, 1944, and arrested after the revolt of July 20. He believed that the most propitious moment for a successful coup d'état had already passed, but he felt that the attempt had to be made, above all to end the war and to spare his country greater misery. He felt that a "resurgence of the conscience" was essential.

The Military Governor of France, General Karl Heinrich von Stülpnagel, shared the convictions of his colleague in Brussels, and labored to advance both theoretical and practical preparations for a change in conditions. Indeed his preparations were more advanced than those of any other headquarters. Karl Heinrich von Stülpnagel was chivalrous by nature and had a great talent for strategy and tactics. The former Chief of the General Staff, General Beck, had selected him to write the masterly manual on *Leadership of Troops*. His political intuition, great military ability, and sure judgment were complemented by a fine sense of proportion. He had been schooled in philosophy and had diplomatic aptitude, which was evident when he was Chief of the "Foreign Armies" (the G-2 or Intelligence) division of the German General Staff, and when he was President of the French Armistice Commission of 1940. He was a German and a European in the best sense. The amorality of the Hitler regime was a constant mental martyrdom to a man of his high ethical principles. Stülpnagel's friendship with Rommel went back to their days under Falkenhausen at the Infantry School at Dresden.

After preliminary discussions by the Chief of Staff, Rommel and Stülpnagel met in a country house in Mareil-Marly near St. Germain on May 15, 1944, together with their Chiefs of Staff, for a comprehensive conference on the necessary measures for ending the war in the west and overthrowing the Nazi regime. The Commander in Chief and the Military Governor reviewed the political and military factors and decided on the theoretical and practical details. They both told the Commander in Chief West, von Rundstedt, of their political anxieties and military problems, and found a ready listener. The Quartermaster General of the Army, Artillery General Eduard Wagner, visited Army Group B in May to co-ordinate the necessary preparations in the west with the planned conspiracy of the High Command of the Army. He told Rommel of the active resistance at the High Command headquarters.

of the timetable for preparing the revolt, and, for the first time, of the attempts that had already been made on the life of Hitler. Rommel objected to the plans to assassinate Hitler. He did not want to make a martyr of him. His idea was to use reliable Panzer formations to seize Hitler, so that he could be brought before a German court and tried for crimes against his own people and against humanity. He should be tried by the people who had elected him.

Important persons came almost daily from the Reich to Rommel's headquarters, where they could talk freely without fear of the Gestapo, and search for a way out of a situation that was becoming more desperate day by day. Among them were Reichsminister Dr. Dorpmüller and the Gauleiter of Hamburg, Kauffmann.

Communications came to Rommel from people of all walks, confirming the decisions that had been taken and showing their trust in Rommel as a man and as a soldier.

The author and philosopher Ernst Jünger, a captain on the staff of the military governor of France, brought a memorandum to Rommel early in May on his peace proposals [1] which he had already worked out during the winter of 1941–42. Rommel was deeply impressed by Jünger's ideas, and particularly with his plan for reconstruction on the basis of a United States of Europe, in a true Christian and humanitarian spirit. The appeal of Jünger in those apocalyptic days with their tremendous pressures had a near-mystic force that won its own disciples.

On April 14, the former mayor, Dr. Goerdeler, had asked Dr. Strölin, Lord Mayor of Stuttgart, to arrange a meeting between Marshal Rommel and the former foreign minister, Constantin von Neurath, whose knowledge of foreign affairs might be utilized.

[1] *The Peace* (Chicago, Henry Regnery Co., 1948).

Rommel respected Baron von Neurath as a diplomat of the old school; because of his aristocratic convictions, Neurath rejected National Socialism. Rommel felt drawn towards this fellow Swabian. Neurath's son had been attached to Rommel's staff in Africa. Since a visit by Rommel to Strölin and Neurath would not have escaped the notice of the Gestapo, he empowered his Chief of Staff to represent him at the meetings with Baron von Neurath and Strölin on May 27, 1944, in Freudenstadt. The meeting served as a medium for an exchange of views between the enemies of Hitler on the western front and those in the homeland. The Chief of Staff first described the military situation in the west with invasion imminent. On behalf of the Field Marshal, he asked what plans those at home might have to save the German people from ruin. Neurath began by reviewing foreign political developments since February 4, 1938, the day when he was removed from office and General von Fritsch removed from command of the Army, and talked of how he had warned Hitler in vain against the policy that he was following. Dr. Strölin gave special attention to Adolf Hitler as the essence of the problem, the man with whom the Allies would never reach any political agreement. Until he was eliminated there could be no new constructive policy. But there would have to be swift action, before invasion, since it was essential to have an unbroken front if all these plans were to be carried out. Strölin thought only Rommel could provide the necessary over-all military leadership, since his sincere nature and soldierly qualities not only made him popular in Germany but had won respect abroad.

Both Neurath and Strölin asked that an urgent appeal be transmitted to the Field Marshal to be ready to assume a role in the deliverance of the Reich, whether as commander in chief of the armed forces, or as interim head of state.

Although two men with remarkable qualities—Colonel General Beck and Lord Mayor Goerdeler—were available for the re-creation of the Reich and the carrying out of the revolt, they did not have the reputation of Rommel, who could win over the people and the Army during the critical beginnings of the revolt, and who would be acceptable to the Allies in negotiations.

The Freudenstadt conversations also touched on the possibilities of getting in contact with the Western Allies through the Vatican, the British Ambassador in Madrid, Sir Samuel Hoare, or through Swiss intermediaries. Feelers had already been put out to the Allies through Rome, Lisbon, and Madrid, but without result.

Ten days later Strölin transmitted a memorandum from Neurath on the foreign political situation and its prospects, which indeed seemed to be very limited.

The elimination of Hitler was discussed at length. It was the opinion of Rommel that Hitler should be arrested and brought before a German court, against which Strölin supported Beck's and Goerdeler's opinion that Hitler should be done away with. They foresaw the latent danger of a civil war if Hitler were left alive.

A broad outline was prepared for explaining the *coup d'état* to the people and the troops.

At a second meeting, links between the opposition groups were strengthened. A means of communication with Rommel's headquarters was devised. It worked well and was never detected.

The Field Marshal approved the substance of the conversations, and let Neurath and Strölin know that he had undertaken preparatory measures and was ready to do his utmost, without making any claim on his part for an office in the new government.

There was an American attempt to contact Rommel that never came to his knowledge, and was revealed only after the war. The American Colonel Smart, shot down over Vienna on May 10, 1944, declared when he was interrogated that he had wanted to get in touch with Rommel in an attempt to arrange for an end to the war. A record of the interrogation was drawn up at the officers' prisoner-of-war camp at Oberursel, and one copy each was sent to Göring, Goebbels, and the Air Ministry. Rommel was not informed—one more example of the methods of concealment practiced by the German leadership, and of the lack of co-operation between the three services.

Every thought in the weeks before invasion centered upon means of saving the Reich. Only the man who has himself to wrestle with decisions that will extend in human, political, and military scope far beyond his own nation and touch the course of history itself, only that man can picture the turmoil that such stresses caused in the conscience of a German military leader. The problems that faced the Prince of Homburg, Prince Louis Ferdinand, and Yorck, can hardly match those that confronted Hitler's generals. Field Marshal Rommel agreed with what Napoleon had demanded of his generals—that in decisive moments in history, statesmanlike thinking must prevail over military thinking. The Field Marshal was no "Philistine general of submissive obedience," as Schlieffen called it, no "special duty" general for Hitler to send forward as Robespierre sent his, the enemy ahead, the noose behind. Rommel held the code of Moltke, which in the last resort put humanity higher than military duty, and man above principle. Rommel liked to quote the writings of Hitler as he strolled in the park of La Roche Guyon in the evening. With bitter irony he repeated from Hitler's *Mein Kampf* the words that stood in sharp contrast to the dictator's later actions.

When the Government of a nation is leading it to its doom, rebellion is not only the right but the duty of every citizen . . . Human laws supersede the laws of the State. . . .
It is the duty of diplomacy to maintain the existence of a nation, not to lead it heroically to destruction. Every means of maintaining it is expedient, and to neglect it must be considered an irresponsible crime.

Rommel struggled to determine at what point obedience must end for a general who feels responsible for the fate of his nation, and at what point human conscience would demand insurrection. He did know the difference between obedience to God and obedience to man. For the sake of the people he must assume an extraordinary burden of responsibility, if all other means were exhausted. Once again he would try by means of written and oral presentations of all his thoughts to persuade Hitler, if possible, to reverse his course. If this last appeal were disregarded, as those preceding it had been, then he would feel released from his oath of loyalty. Then it would be his duty to take action— action for his fatherland. It was clear to him that only the highest military leader was qualified, entitled, and obliged to undertake this metaphysical responsibility and decision, not the individual soldier or officer who could not possess the same high degree of insight. Rommel accepted personal responsibility for decisions and rejected Hitler's demand that he be responsible only for executing orders. He wanted to save his country and the world from further bloodshed and protect the beautiful towns of his homeland from extinction, and its fertile fields from desolation. Never would he permit the battle to be waged on German soil, no matter how severe the conditions of a merciless enemy might be. Talleyrand had once said: "Blessed be the people who can find a peacemaker, when their own leader is not acceptable even as the bearer of a white flag."

Rommel was quite aware that independent action might lead to self-destruction, and possibly be a pretext for a new legend of "the stab in the back," but he never recoiled from the thought of personal sacrifice.

Rommel, von Falkenhausen, and von Stülpnagel quite openly informed Marshal von Rundstedt of their discussions and plans.

There was mutual trust between Rommel, Rundstedt, and General Blumentritt, Rundstedt's chief of staff. Rommel deeply respected Rundstedt as an experienced soldier of the old school, a famous pupil of Schlieffen. In their judgment of the over-all conduct of the war and the political situation, the two marshals were in complete agreement. Rundstedt was an eminent strategist, a master of the tools of war, but in the last years of the war he had lost, with advancing age, his creative drive and his clear sense of responsibility to the nation. Sarcastic resignation and indifference became more and more noticeable in him. Of course he despised Hitler, and referred to him in all private conversations, as Hindenburg did, by the nickname "the Bohemian corporal." But he seemed to think that the height of wisdom was to make representations and grave reports. He left action to others. During a discussion on the formulation of joint demands to Hitler, Rundstedt said to Rommel: "You are young. You know and love the people. You do it."

It was not only as a general but also as a personality that Rundstedt became resigned, and at a time when supreme efforts were demanded. Because of his increasing rigidity, Rundstedt remained almost unknown to the soldier at the front, while Rommel ceaselessly exerted his remarkable powers of leadership on the soldiers personally, not sparing himself, being a veritable "Promachos."

Field Marshal von Rundstedt told Rommel on the afternoon of July 4, 1944, on being recalled from the west, that he would never again accept a command. It is difficult to explain his subsequent behavior: he sat on the so-called Court of Honor after July 20, which by expelling his comrades from the Wehrmacht created the grounds on which they were convicted by the People's Court; he resumed the western command again on September 5, and finally he represented Hitler at the "state funeral" for the murdered Erwin Rommel on October 17 at Ulm. Here destiny gave him the unique chance to play the role of Mark Antony. He remained in his moral apathy.

The conclusions of these conferences were embodied in a timetable for mobilization, worked out with considerable help from General Karl Heinrich von Stülpnagel. In outline form it called for:

In the West: Definition of the premises under which an armistice could be concluded with Generals Eisenhower and Montgomery *without* participation by Hitler. Field Marshal Rommel thought of sending as his negotiators General Karl Heinrich von Stülpnagel, General Baron Leo Geyr von Schweppenburg, Lieutenant General Hans Speidel, Lieutenant General Count Gerd von Schwerin, Vice-Admiral Friedrich Ruge, and Lieutenant Colonel Cäsar von Hofacker.

The bases foreseen for negotiating an armistice were:

German evacuation of the occupied western territories

and withdrawal behind the Westwall. Surrender of the administration of the occupied territories to the Allies. *Immediate suspension of the Allied bombing of Germany.* Armistice, not unconditional surrender, followed by negotiations for peace to bring about order and prevent chaos. Field Marshal Rommel expected that the Allies would give them such an opportunity. Appeal to the German people from all radio stations in the Western Command, frankly revealing the true political and military situation and its causes, and describing Hitler's criminal conduct of State affairs. Informing the troops of the measures necessary to avert a catastrophe.

The Home Front: Arrest of Hitler for trial before a German court by the resistance forces in the High Command of the Army, or rather by Panzer forces to be brought up for this purpose. Field Marshal Rommel continued to hold the view that Hitler should not be removed by assassination but should be brought before German judges. Overthrow of the National Socialist rule by force. Temporary assumption of executive power in Germany by the resistance forces of all classes under the leadership of General Beck, Lord Mayor Dr. Goerdeler, and the former Hessian Minister of the Interior and trade-union leader, Leuschner.

Field Marshal Rommel did not personally aspire to the leadership of the Reich, but was ready to take over command of the army or the Wehrmacht.

No military dictatorship. Domestic conciliation and no strife. Preparation of a constructive peace within the framework of a United States of Europe. Co-operation with all who were willing to work for reconstruction.

In the East: Continuation of the fight. Holding a shortened line between the mouth of the Danube, the Carpathian mountains, Lemberg (Lwów), the Vistula, and the

Memel. Immediate evacuation of Courland (Lithuania) and other "fortresses."

The preparations had to be speeded up so that action could be taken *before* an invasion began. For all negotiations a firm western front was a prerequisite. The stability of the western front was, therefore, our constant concern.

iv

THE INVASION

TIME AFTER TIME Hitler postponed his long-promised visit to the western front. Rommel wanted to inform him in person without fail, before the invasion, of his views on the military and political situation and insist that certain political measures be taken. After consultation with Marshal von Rundstedt, he telephoned to Hitler's adjutant, Lieutenant General Schmundt, and arranged for a personal interview with Hitler on June 6. He left by car for Obersalzberg on the morning of June 5—it was expressly forbidden for senior officers to use aircraft for travel, as it was impossible to protect them against the Allied air forces. Rommel intended to spend the night of June 5–6 at Herrlingen, near Ulm, with his family.

June 5 was a quiet day. The Commander in Chief of the western forces circulated the reports of our agents, as had happened often in the past, that invasion was possible between June 6 and 15. Code messages were intercepted naming several different dates and then reporting postponement of the date of invasion. There was a noticeable increase in activities of the Free French resistance movement in the interior of France, principally the distribution in Brittany of leaflets calling upon the people to begin active resistance to the Germans. Army Group B had been in a state of preparedness on the entire front since the beginning of June.

The Fifteenth German Army intercepted a code message on June 5 at 10:00 P.M. indicating that the invasion was to begin.

As a matter of course, the Fifteenth Army immediately alerted its own troops and informed the armies on either side of it. The Commander in Chief West, to whom the message was relayed by phone, decided that he would not alert the whole front.

German air and naval reconnaissance had not been effective for several days previous because of Allied air activity. Naval patrols did not put to sea on the evening of June 5 because of "heavy seas."

The Chief of Staff of Army Group B received reports in the first hours of the morning of June 6 that enemy parachute troops had dropped in the vicinity of Caen and the southeastern area of the Cotentin peninsula. It was not at all clear at first whether these were airborne landings in strength or just groups of parachutists dropped to provide a link between the French resistance forces and the invasion forces. Between the Seine and the Orne especially, the parachute landings were scattered over a wide area. In spite of this uncertainty, the Army Group ordered all units to battle stations. Between 3:00 and 4:00 A.M. the reports of parachute landings became more numerous. Then there followed bombing of coastal defenses, and the approach of strong Allied air forces was detected. The Panzer divisions in reserve were ordered to be ready to move. The Headquarters of the I SS Panzer Corps, which was not under the command of the Army Group, was requested to keep in contact with General Erich Marcks, commanding the corps on the Calvados coast and the Cotentin peninsula, and with the forward Panzer divisions. The 21st Panzer Division received orders to move up to its prepared positions south of Caen. The High Command of the Armed Forces and the Commander in Chief of the western forces were notified.

At 5:30 A.M., all of a sudden, the bombardment of the Calvados coast by hundreds of ships' guns began. The previously prepared automatic defense measures were put into operation. The prearranged orders for "Operation Normandy" were issued.

The Chief of Staff of Army Group B reported by telephone to his Commander in Chief at Herrlingen between 6:00 and 6:30 A.M. on the events and on the first steps taken. Marshal Rommel gave his approval. He at once canceled his trip to Berchtesgaden and was back at his battle headquarters in La Roche Guyon between 4:00 and 5:00 P.M.

It was impossible to issue strategic orders in the early hours of the invasion, before reconnaissance reports had produced a clear picture of enemy movements. We could do nothing but wait patiently. Continuous telephone calls from the headquarters of the Supreme Command and from that of the Commander in Chief West (von Rundstedt) indicated that both these headquarters were exceptionally nervous. The situation was explained to General Jodl several times by the Chief of Staff in telephone conversations, and he also asked the High Command to release its Panzer reserve divisions. After 6:00 A.M. more reports of troop landings on the beaches came in. These reports all came from Army sources; no German aircraft could reach the Normandy area. On June 6, the Allied air forces had already prevented the Luftwaffe's available force of 70 bombers and 90 fighters from leaving the ground and had made their

airfields unusable. It was apparent by afternoon that the
brunt of a large-scale landing had fallen on the coastal sector between the Orne and Vire rivers. The situation between the Seine and the Orne was unclear, and in the southeast corner of the Cotentin peninsula the strength of Allied
airborne landings was unknown.

Anticipating that every hour would count in the struggle
to destroy the first enemy lodgments and to prevent him
from reinforcing and strengthening his foothold, Rommel
had, as early as May, given a battle order to the 21st Panzer
Division, stationed south of Caen, that the momentary
weakness of the enemy just after landing should be utilized
for an automatic counterattack. Every possibility had been
prepared for, taking into account the terrain and the available forces. The 21st Panzer Division had been stationed
by Rommel at this vital point, but he had been denied
additional Panzer forces. When Rommel spoke on the telephone from Herrlingen on the morning of D Day, he again
told his Chief of Staff that the counterattack of the 21st
Panzer Division would probably be necessary and ordered
that all available reserves in the divisional area should be
concentrated under one command. After Hitler had refused repeated demands for the release of additional armored reserves, the 21st Panzer Division, at 10:00 A.M. on
June 6, moved forward along both banks of the Orne to
launch a counterattack. The command was given by General Marcks, commanding general of the LXXXIV Army
Corps. The armored thrust reached the coast and established
contact with the remnants of the 716th Division still holding out in strong points. The enemy then dropped airborne
troops in among the attacking Panzer units and in the area
east of Caen. The divisional commander took the independent decision to break off the attack and free the rear
of the division. This decision rendered a distinct service to

the Allies, and it prevented the exploitation of the initial success of the counterattack. The use of airborne troops against these Panzer forces proved how much the 21st Panzer attack had disturbed the Allied command. Field Marshal Rommel had repeatedly and unsuccessfully asked during the previous month for the I SS Panzer Corps with the 12th SS Panzer Division "Hitler Youth," and the Panzer-Lehr Division, intending to place them between Caen and Falaise. He planned to renew this demand to Hitler on June 6. If the Panzer Corps, with the three divisions, had been thrown in immediately, there might have been important local successes at the moment of weakness during the enemy landing.

By the evening of D Day the Allies, aided by their air and naval superiority, were able to establish a bridgehead between the Orne and the area north of Ryes fifteen miles broad and up to six miles deep. A second bridgehead was established in the southeast corner of the Cotentin peninsula nine miles long and two miles deep.

The British Second Army under General Dempsey had landed an airborne division and between four and five armored or infantry divisions on the Calvados coast. The U. S. First Army under General Hodges had landed two airborne divisions and three to four armored divisions on the Cotentin peninsula. The German 716th and 353rd Divisions held out bravely in their trenches and battle stations under a hail of fire from sea and air and then from land, of a previously unknown intensity. A ring of very heavy artillery fire from the Allied navies cut off the battle area from the rest of France. The Allied air forces made some 25,000 sorties during D Day. Without having actually experienced the force of the land, sea, and air bombardment one cannot judge its destructive effect on morale; but Hitler would not acknowledge it, in spite of the many oral and written reports he received. He reacted at first with shabby reproaches and suspicious interference with the counter-measures. He cast about for scapegoats and thought of dis-missing a number of commanders; Rommel, however, shielded them.

The I SS Panzer Corps was finally released on June 6 about 3:00 P.M., but it could not be moved during daylight because of enemy air supremacy. It seemed by that evening that the Allies were concentrating the weight of their at-tack between the Orne and the Vire. In all probability they intended a thrust at Paris.

The Command of the I SS Panzer Corps took over the Caen sector early on June 7 with orders to carry out the same attack that the 21st Panzer Division had unsuccess-fully attempted on the previous day. It was to use the com-bined forces of the 21st, the 12th SS, and the Panzer-Lehr divisions. The enemy was to be dislodged from the Caen-Bayeux area. The timing and direction of the counterattack were worked out in detail, but the shortness of the June night prevented the German armored units and their sup-ply columns from being moved up in time. Waves of bomber attacks on roads and crossroads made all movement impossible.

It was not until June 9 that the counterattack of the I SS Panzer Corps was carried out. The third day of landing operations was over, and the critical moment for the enemy was past. Saturation bombing and sustained naval gunfire had prevented the I SS Panzer Corps from assembling in time in the area south of Caen. There were heavy German losses in men and matériel, particularly in signal equipment. The problems of command were made still more difficult, for without air cover we had only meager means of observ-ing enemy movements. The German attack encountered an opponent ready to defend himself and superior in ground

5. An American Antitank Unit in Action

forces also. After local successes the advance towards the coast was halted.

By this time the British Second Army already had about ten motorized and armored divisions in the Calvados bridgehead; the American First Army, eight to nine divisions on the Cotentin peninsula. The Allies had linked up their landing points by seizing the area north and west of Bayeux. They increased their strength more rapidly than German reserves could be brought up. Without any air support, German units had to move at some distance away from the roads, which in many places were blocked or disrupted by bombing. There was an uncanny precision in the co-operation between the Allied land forces and their air and naval support, as the first three days of the invasion had shown.

During the rapidly developing situation between June 6 and June 8, Army Group B made the following urgent requests to the Commander in Chief West.

The immediately available forces of the Fifteenth Army should be moved southward across the Seine on the afternoon of June 7; any movement by the Commander in Chief of the Army Group of even one division in his own command was strictly prohibited by the High Command.

It was also proposed to thin the garrisons of the Channel coast. The eight infantry divisions in the Fifteenth Army, which were drawn up in deep defensive positions, were to be moved by night marches—the railways were destroyed and there was no motor transport available—toward the Normandy front to relieve the Panzer divisions and release them for more mobile operations.

This proposal was at first turned down. Only much later —and too late—was hesitant and piecemeal approval received. The reason for refusal was that Hitler and the High Command expected a second Allied landing on the Channel coast. This question of a second landing was to play an important part in the first six weeks of the invasion.

Marshal Rommel considered a second landing rather unlikely for strategic, tactical, and political reasons. But the bits of intelligence data that came to us from above during the next five weeks reported between 30 and 50 divisions still in the British Isles. Of course, in over-all strategy these forces had to be taken into account. Rommel indicated the stretch of coast between the Somme and the Seine as the sector they might possibly invade. From the middle of June on, Army Group B thought it unlikely that Patton's Army would land north of the Seine, and certainly not on the strongly fortified Channel coast, since the Allies had established adequate bridgeheads in the Orne-Vire and Cotentin areas which were about to be linked. The High Command again refused to let divisions of the Fifteenth Army be brought up and did not allow any freedom of operation. General Jodl later called this decision a mistake. It was not until the second half of July that the High Command ordered the inactive divisions of the Fifteenth Army from the Normandy sector of the Channel coast. But by that time it was questionable whether these troops would not have been better employed preparing a Seine defense line, even if it was still intended to renounce any freedom of maneuver in the west.

Field Marshal Rommel also demanded that the bulk of the divisions in Brittany and the Channel Islands be withdrawn and brought to the Normandy front. In Brittany it would suffice to secure the coast; it was strategically impossible to hold the peninsula. Brittany had lost its importance as a naval base; the U-boats were reduced in numbers and limited in effectiveness. Subsequent events proved that Rommel was right in this demand.

On the Channel Islands alone there were the 319th Division, reinforced by a Panzer regiment, a flak brigade, and other units, totaling 35,000 men, who had to surrender in May 1945 without a fight. The ordinary soldiers with their prophetic instinct had nicknamed the 319th "the Canada division"—it seemed destined to end up in prisoner-of-war camps. After rejecting in writing Rommel's demands, Hitler forbade any further suggestions of this nature.

Another of Rommel's demands was that the Mediterranean front in France should be abandoned, since "one cannot hold everything," and the LVIII Panzer Corps, stationed in the south of France, be brought north with its four Panzer divisions (the 9th and 11th Panzer divisions, and the 2nd and 17th SS Panzer divisions). The process of regrouping them and bringing them up to strength had just started. Hitler and the High Command, fearful of a landing on the Mediterranean coast, refused this proposal also. These Panzer divisions were finally brought up in July and August, but to a then strategically unsound area, the area south of the Seine.

It ought to have been quite clear that the Mediterranean coast, with its weak garrison and open coasts, would not have been equal to a serious attack. But if that coast were invaded as well, strategy on a large scale would be necessary—all of southern France would have to be abandoned, the forces in the west withdrawn behind the Seine-Yonne line, and all possible reserves assembled in the rear of the east flank.

Neither the Commander in Chief for the West nor the High Command would approve these demands. Rommel was told that such matters were not within his competence, and once more all strategic planning was forbidden.

Thus the first phase of the invasion ended with an obvious military, political, and psychological success for the Allies. They had overcome the difficulties of the first few critical days, without any notable reverses, because of the reliable co-operation of the three services and because of the great effectiveness of their new technical equipment. They had consolidated their position. It had become apparent to us that they could be dislodged or contained in their bridgeheads for any length of time only if strong German air and naval forces could be brought to bear. The tactical failure of the counterattack could not be ascribed to negligence in the field command or to reluctance to fight on the part of the troops. It was due solely to the effectiveness of the enemy air and naval forces. In the first days of the invasion they had succeeded in bringing about a serious shortage of fuel and ammunition on the German side.

From June 9 on, the initiative lay with the Allies.

1

The Period from June 9 to August 24

DURING this six-week period the Germans made every effort to drive the Allies from their bridgeheads into the sea.

The Western Panzer Group, quartered in Paris, commanded by General Baron Geyr von Schweppenburg, was brought up on June 7, at the urgent request of Army Group B. But it was the evening of June 8 before this group was ready to take over the area east of the Orne to the Tilly sector. Troops located on the inner flanks of the Fifteenth and Seventh armies and the I SS Panzer Corps stationed in this area were put under the command of von Schweppenburg. His battle orders were to use all available armored forces to throw the enemy off the mainland. After the failure of the I SS Panzer Corps, General von Schweppenburg took time to prepare a careful counter-offensive for the night of June 10-11.

After these orders had been given at Panzer Group Headquarters, with the Commander in Chief of the Army Group present, the Panzer-Lehr Division reported an enemy breakthrough from the west. It was one of those exaggerated reports that inevitably occur in war, but it made countermeasures necessary. Shortly after this report was received, the headquarters staff of the Western Panzer Group was practically wiped out by saturation bombing. Probably signals from the newly installed headquarters short-wave equipment had been picked up and pinpointed by the Allies. The Panzer Group lost its Chief of Staff, General von Dawans, and the IA, its operations officer, as well as other officers. The communications system was put out of commission. Only the Commander in Chief, who was slightly wounded, and a few of his staff escaped. It was not until June 26 that he could resume his duties with a new staff, hampered by all the drawbacks of improvisation.

There was no determined counteroffensive on the days following June 11, since the Panzer forces, under steadily increasing pressure from the British armored divisions, were forced to take the defensive. Hitler and the High Command interfered daily with the field commanders and as usual wanted to deal with all the enemy's operations simultaneously. An avalanche of nervous orders descended from Supreme Headquarters. We were ordered to thwart the enemy attack southwards past Caen, to prevent a push southwards from Bayeux, to hold Cherbourg at all costs, to frustrate the encirclement of the Cotentin peninsula and enemy operations against Brittany. Finally an order came through from the Führer that the bridgehead between the Orne and the Vire was to be "destroyed" section by section. This order even went into details as to the use of a mortar brigade east of the Orne. But all these instructions

were to be carried out without the necessary ground reserves and without air or naval support.

While these events were taking place between the Orne
and the Vire, where the weight of the Allied attack seemed
to be in the Caen-Bayeux area, the Americans sought to
strengthen and extend their bridgeheads in the southeast of
the Cotentin peninsula. German forces fighting against the
American bridgehead included parts of the 243rd, the 91st
and 77th Divisions, the 3rd Parachute Division, part of the
17th SS Panzer Grenadiers, and the 30th Brigade. Yet, although General Marcks proceeded prudently, no concentrated counteroffensive developed for the same reasons as
those which had prevented a successful attack in the Caen
sector. The reserve units arrived singly, and it had been impossible to build up an offensive force with effective striking power. For example: the scattered 12th SS Panzer Division arrived at the battle area in the course of June 7; the
Panzer-Lehr Division on June 8 and 9; the 346th Infantry
Division on June 8 and 9; the 77th Infantry Division on
June 11; the 2nd Panzer Division on June 13; the 3rd Parachute Division on June 13; and the 1st SS Panzer Division on June 18. Mechanized artillery units, mortar brigades, and other special troops came up in the same fashion,
or in a still more irregular fashion, because the railways
were being increasingly destroyed.

Only if the coastal sectors north and south of Normandy
had been ruthlessly stripped of their garrisons could we
have to some extent counterbalanced the advantages that
the Allies enjoyed as a result of their air supremacy. This
was not done, because the High Command estimate of enemy intentions was based on the supposition that a second
landing was imminent.

The force of the counteroffensive on the Cotentin peninsula was spent in isolated thrusts, and most of the reinforce-

ments were used up for defensive operations as they arrived, because of the suddenly developing crises in the battle.

Bad weather on June 9 and 10 had somewhat reduced Allied air activities, but the defense could not take advantage of this respite.

It was becoming obvious that the American command intended to cut off the peninsula and then capture Cherbourg. In his directives Hitler indicated that it was "decisive for the war" to hold Cherbourg. But the fortress of Cherbourg was neither properly fortified against an attack from the land side, nor was there a large enough garrison for defense. High Command orders designated four divisions for the defense of Cherbourg—the 709th, the 91st, the 247th and the 77th. They were ordered to "hold the enemy as long as possible" in the bridgehead on the eastern coast and then "fight their way back to Cherbourg." Although Rommel protested repeatedly, these orders were never revoked. In carrying out this mission, the infantry divisions, not mobile enough and not properly supplied, were overrun during their retreat by Allied armored units and were largely destroyed by air forces. Such an extended land and sea front was not tenable without sufficient troops and without any air cover or naval support. The Army Group supported the views of the LXXXIV Corps and the Seventh Army— that the German forces on the Cotentin peninsula ought to be so situated that they could be saved from destruction by being withdrawn southward. But these possibilities were sacrificed to the illusory idea of defending Cherbourg. Always the same orders echoed from Germany: "Hold your ground. Do not yield a step."

As a result of the orders and counterorders of the German High Command, the Americans broke through at Saint Sauveur, and caused the loss of nearly four German divisions. Then Rommel decided on his own initiative to

withdraw southward all forces within reach and seal off the
Cotentin peninsula. A fighting group of the 77th Infantry
Division, under Colonel Bacherer, succeeded in a bold
breakthrough toward the south, and closed a gap in the
Cotentin front. The city and port of Cherbourg fell on
June 25, and by June 30 the last German pockets of re-
sistance had to give up the fight.

The capture of the port of Cherbourg was not so vital
for supplying the Allied forces as the Germans had originally supposed. The invention of the artificial harbors and
their use on the Calvados coast were of decisive significance. The moral effect of the surrender of Cherbourg was
more serious. But in spite of all advantages, the Allies had
not reached their objectives in the time limits they had set
for themselves. A captured American map marked with
dates and objectives for the invasion army showed that the
Allies had expected Cherbourg to fall on June 6, and the
Americans to have reached the Domfront-Avranches line
on June 10. The operations were progressing considerably
slower than the American commander in chief had calculated, and they required a greater number of troops.

After Cherbourg had fallen and the Allied battle units
had been released, the Army Group expected the American First Army to shift the center of attack to the St.
Lô-Carentan area, and take the Coutances-St. Lô line, to be
used as a line of departure from which it would break
through southwards and from which it would establish contact with Montgomery's army group in Normandy.

The British Second Army had not perceived a wide and
dangerous gap near Bayeux that yawned in the German
front for many days. A breakthrough south- and southeastward would have been decisively important even then
and might have brought about the collapse of the German
front south of the Seine. Instead, the British offensive was

directed eastward in order to cut the German front into ribbons by a "simple frontal attack." With all available reserves being utilized, the gap south of Bayeux was closed by the newly arrived XXXXVII Panzer Corps of General Baron von Funk, consisting of General Baron von Lüttwitz' 2nd Panzer division and General Bayerlein's Panzer-Lehr division.

Because of enemy air and naval superiority, the whole defensive battle was consuming German strength, since Hitler had forbidden any kind of elastic strategy and had insisted that every inch of ground be defended. Thus the tactically worthless foothold across the Orne near Caen was held only by grievous losses of men.

This tactical patchwork left all the initiative to the enemy, and was unsound in every respect.

THE MARGIVAL CONFERENCE WITH ADOLF HITLER
ON JUNE 17

Such was our predicament when Hitler at last decided to accede to the continual urgings of Marshals von Rundstedt and Rommel and visit the western front, so that he could receive firsthand information, and, if he thought it necessary, make new strategic decisions. An unexpected telephone call on the evening of June 16 ordered both field marshals and their chiefs of staff to be at Battle Headquarters "W II" at Margival, north of Soissons, at 9:00 A.M. on June 17, to make a report to Hitler. Rommel had to drive 140 miles to the rear immediately after returning at 3:00. A.M. from a twenty-one hour tour of the Cotentin front. There was no time to make any preparations for this conference.

The Führer's headquarters "W II" had been built in 1940 on historic soil. Only a short distance away stood the cross at "Laffaux Corner," which commemorated the place where

the front in the first World War turned sharply northward
away from its east–west direction. From this point the
Chemin des Dames, bitterly contested in both World Wars,
runs eastward between the Aisne and the Oise-Aisne canal.
The Margival headquarters was situated five miles north-
east of Soissons, where the railway leading to Laon passed
through a cut beside the mouth of a tunnel that was con-
venient for concealing Hitler's special train. At the headquarters there were roomy, well-camouflaged concrete
bunkers. The mess stood on an elevation, with a fine view
of the Cathedral at Soissons. The Führer's bunker contained a large working room on the ground level, sleeping
quarters with bath, rooms for adjutants, and special air
raid shelters equipped for work and rest. This was to have
been the command headquarters for the invasion of Britain
in 1940, but it had never been used until June 17, 1944. For
this conference it was guarded and hermetically sealed off
by the SS Escort Commandos of the Führer.

Hitler, together with General Jodl and his entourage,
arrived in the early morning of June 17 from Metz.
He had flown from Berchtesgaden to Metz and motored
from there to the headquarters. He looked pale and sleep-
less, playing nervously with his glasses and an array of col-
ored pencils which he held between his fingers. He sat
hunched upon a stool, while the field marshals stood. His
hypnotic powers seemed to have waned. There was a curt
and frosty greeting from Hitler, who then in a loud voice
spoke bitterly of his displeasure at the success of the Allied
landings, for which he tried to hold the field commanders
responsible. He ordered that the "fortress of Cherbourg"
be held at all costs.

Field Marshal von Rundstedt, after a few introductory
words, turned the discussion over to Rommel as the commander in chief at the invasion front. Rommel with merci-

less frankness pointed out the crucial aspects of the defense: he had foretold before June 6, and repeated daily since, that the struggle was hopeless against such tremendous superiority in the air, at sea, and on land. After the failure of the German Luftwaffe and naval reconnaissance, the Allies, with overwhelming artillery support, had succeeded in landing by air and sea on the weakly fortified and poorly manned Calvados coast and the Cotentin peninsula. The German divisions engaged at the coast had not been "caught napping" as was reported in an enemy communiqué which was taken at its face value by the German High Command. These divisions had in fact fought to the last breath in their weakly fortified defenses. In this unequal contest both officers and men had battled with superhuman endurance. Rommel presented his estimate of the tactical situation on the Cotentin peninsula and compared the strength of the defense with that of the attack. He then predicted the fall of Cherbourg practically to the day, and demanded that the battle be conducted in accordance with the needs of the hour.

This brought up the whole question of "fortresses"—that is, towns and fortified areas with improvised field fortifications—one of Hitler's pet ideas. Rommel declared that they were useless. He warned against a senseless waste of men and matériel, but he warned in vain. For the course of the invasion and subsequent operations, Hitler declared these places to be "fortresses": Ijmuiden, Walcheren Island, Dunkirk, Calais, Cap Gris Nez, Boulogne, Dieppe, Le Havre, Cherbourg, St. Malo, Brest, Lorient, St. Nazaire, La Pallice, Royan, and the mouth of the Gironde. They tied up 200,000 men and valuable equipment. But the Allies did not bother with these "fortresses," and they did not even cause the Allies to immobilize substantial forces. They fell, some as late as May 1945, after the unconditional surrender of

Germany. Their garrisons were taken prisoner. Hitler had learned nothing from the experiences of Stalingrad, Tunis, the Crimea, or Tarnopol.

Then Marshal Rommel explained what he thought the Allied intentions might be: a breakthrough from the Caen-Bayeux area and the Cotentin peninsula, at first toward the south and then in the direction of Paris; a secondary operation past Avranches to cut off Brittany.

The Allied Twenty-first Army Group under Eisenhower, with its unified command over both British and American forces, had already landed between 22 and 25 armored and mobile divisions, of which 11 or 12 were British and 10 to 12 were American. Two or three additional divisions kept arriving each week. The relative strength of the German forces was such that a successful defense in the west could not be counted on. Therefore the outcome for the western front could not be predicted, and there was no Seine defense line, nor for that matter any other fortified line. The Allied commanders might seem slow and ponderous, but their methodical perseverance and over-all superiority made their success all the more certain.

Rommel no longer believed that a second big landing would be made north of the Seine, and he repeated his demand for unrestricted freedom to operate in the west and for the assignment of first-class Panzer forces, air cover, and naval support. His most urgent need, he said, was for a directive to deal with the expected breakthrough of the American First Army to the west coast of the Cotentin peninsula, and the withdrawal of the Caen front behind the Orne. Field Marshal von Rundstedt supported these demands.

Hitler could not see the truth of this estimate of the enemy position and the day-to-day decline of the strength of the German forces. He prophesied in a strange mixture of cynicism and false intuition, during an endless flow of auto-suggestive phrases, that the "V weapon," which had been put into use on June 16, would be decisive against Great Britain.

He interrupted the conference to dictate to a representative of the Reich press chief the wording of a communiqué announcing the first use of the V weapon, for release to the press and radio. The conference from which the two field marshals had expected so much seemed to be suffocating in an irrelevant monologue of Hitler. The field marshals asked that the V bombs be directed against the Allied bridgeheads in Normandy instead of the British Isles.

The Commanding General of V weapons, Artillery General Heinemann, was summoned and had to point out that the margin of error of these missiles was large; they might fall nine to twelve miles from their targets. Therefore, German troops in the bridgehead areas would be endangered. It was technically impossible, he said, to launch guided missiles at the Allied armies on the mainland. Hitler turned down the proposal that the V weapons be aimed at the ports in southern England, where personnel and supplies for the invasion forces were being transshipped. He declared that he wanted to hit London and make "the English willing to make peace."

The marshals drew his attention again to the failures of the Luftwaffe. Hitler answered that he had been "deceived" by the Command of the Luftwaffe and its technical advisers. Too many types of aircraft had been developed simultaneously without practical results.

Hitler doubted the shocking account that Rommel gave of the destructive power of the enemy's weapons, whereupon Rommel brusquely pointed out that no person of authority from the Führer's headquarters, the High Command, the Luftwaffe, or the Navy had come to the front to form an opinion on the spot regarding the over-all tactical situation and the effect of these weapons. Instead, orders were worked out around the conference table, and there was lacking an evaluation based on front-line knowledge. Rommel exclaimed, "You demand our confidence, but you do not trust us yourself." Hitler flushed at this reproach, but he remained silent.

General Jodl spoke next, indicating what new units of the army, navy, and air force were to be brought up to the front, and the times of their arrival. Hitler talked about the time when "masses of jet fighters" would be thrown in to shatter the air supremacy of the Allies over the front and over Germany. He also mentioned an increase in the use of V bombs, described the military situation in the east and southeast as stabilized, and lost himself in phrases which had to do with the imminent collapse of Britain under V bombs and jet-fighter attacks.

The announced approach of Allied aircraft made it necessary for the conference to be adjourned to the Führer's air-raid shelter. There was only room for Hitler, the two field marshals, and their chiefs of staff, and Hitler's chief adjutant, General Schmundt. Rommel used this opportunity to drop the military discussion and enter into a relentless exposition of the political situation. He predicted that the German front in Normandy would collapse and that a breakthrough into Germany by the Allies could not be checked. The front in Italy would crumble away—Rome had been lost on June 4—and he doubted whether the Russian front could be held. He pointed to Germany's complete political isolation, which would lead to a fatal weakening, the German propaganda line to the contrary. He concluded his critical examination of the situation with an urgent request that the war be brought to an end. Hitler, who had interrupted him several times, cut Rommel off abruptly by saying, "Don't you worry about the future course of the war, but rather about your own invasion front."

Testifying on June 6, 1946, before the Inter-Allied Military Tribunal in Nuremberg, General Jodl said, "Several generals, among them Rommel and von Rundstedt, tried to explain to Hitler the critical position of Germany; but he paid no attention whatsoever to their warnings."

Under the circumstances, both field marshals pointed to the compelling necessity to at last treat France differently, and especially to eliminate the Sauckel program and the influence of the Secret Police of the SS. Hitler also rejected this suggestion.

The gulf between Field Marshal Rommel and Hitler had widened. Hitler's mistrust, indeed his hatred, seemed to have grown. The conference at Margival lasted from 9:00 A.M. to 4:00 P.M., interrupted only for lunch, a one-dish meal at which Hitler bolted a heaped plate of rice and vegetables, after it had been previously tasted for him. Pills and liqueur glasses containing various medicines were ranged around his place, and he took them in turn. Two SS men stood guard behind his chair.

Before the conference ended, Hitler's chief adjutant, General Schmundt, apparently impressed by Rommel's repeated warnings that the High Command had to have first-hand knowledge of the front, requested the Chief of Staff of Army Group B to prepare for a visit on June 19 by Hitler to La Roche Guyon or some other suitable headquarters. Field commanders of all ranks and services were to be notified, and were to report personally on their problems. These arrangements were immediately made. On the way back from Soissons to La Roche Guyon, the Military Governor of France, General von Stülpnagel, was informed of the results of the conference at Margival. The Chief of

Staff telephoned early on June 18 to General Blumentritt at St. Germain to arrange details regarding the time of Hitler's visit to the front. He was told the incredible news that Hitler had returned to Berchtesgaden on the night of June 17-18. The cause of the hasty return was that a V bomb had fallen on the Führer's headquarters at Margival on June 17, just after the two field marshals had left. A defective gyro steering mechanism had set several V bombs on an easterly course after they had been launched from their coastal bases. They had not done much damage and, although the bomb had fallen near the Führer's air-raid shelter, it had no effect and there were no casualties.

The destructiveness of the "miracle weapon"—the V-1— was indeed minimal in comparison to the effort of producing it. News from England and the evidence of British prisoners of war confirmed this.

The "discussion with the Führer" at Margival was highly destructive in its military, political, and psychological consequences. The promises of Hitler that he would send up reinforcements, especially air forces, were never kept. Contrary to Hitler's confident statement of June 17, on June 20 the Soviet full-scale offensive against the Central Army Group began and smashed its front on both sides of the Smolensk-Minsk paved automobile highway. After breaking the front, the Soviet divisions rolled forward without meeting resistance, towards the very borders of the Reich itself. All available German reserves of the High Command, especially the home guard, were streaming toward the east to stem the flood; it was again impossible to get a clear report on the actual situation from the High Command.

Towards the end of June, the British Second Army in Normandy seemed to be massing its forces for a concentric attack on Caen in order to break through in the direction

of Paris and win sufficient ground to carry out strategic
maneuvers. German losses mounted daily, particularly as a
result of naval gunfire controlled by air observation planes.
The Allies had more than three hundred ships bombarding
the coast, and air bombing was ceaseless. Hitler had forbidden any withdrawal from the small and unimportant
bridgehead across the Orne at Caen. This had been suggested on June 17 since some of our best fighting units
were being inexorably ground to bits there. In the middle
of June the II SS Panzer Corps was brought up from Hungary under the command of SS Chief Group Leader Bit-
trich to assume the burden of battle at Caen and ease the
pressure generally on the Normandy front. Because of the
destruction of railway lines, part of this corps had to de-
train east of Paris and march the rest of the way. It was
put under the command of the reorganized Western Panzer Group. This group was supposed to make a deep flank
and rear attack on the enemy fighting at Caen with its
whole concentrated strength of three Panzer corps (I, II SS,
and XXXXVII). It was to cut the British off from the sea
and destroy them. But the attack could not be launched
with the desired resolution or strength, not only because
one defensive crisis after another arose at the front, but
also because the enemy artillery fire and bombing attacks
were too overpowering. The divisions of the I SS and the
XXXXVII Panzer corps could not be relieved by infantry
divisions, in part because air attacks prevented the infantry
units from arriving in time, and in part because their equipment, organization, and leadership were not equal to those
of the mobile armored divisions of the enemy. The British
divisions, supported by all kinds of firepower, were able to
shift the main effort of their attack with lightning rapidity.
    The attack of the II SS Panzer Corps, consisting of the
9th and 10th Panzer Divisions, was eventually carried out

without much support from other divisions. It ran into the concentric fire of the enemy and foundered on June 29 and 30 under the gunfire of tanks, field and heavy artillery, naval bombardment, and air bombing. The II Panzer Corps failed to achieve its objective, but had at least stabilized the front locally. Hitler accused these divisions of lacking willingness to fight, experience, and ability. This was unfair; the corps did as much as it could. These newly brought-up troops also began to lose strength and battle effectiveness at an ever increasing rate.

It had been the intention of the German command that the infantry divisions should relieve the Panzer divisions, so that the latter might be used for a strategic role in a more mobile warfare. This intention was contradictory to Hitler's previous orders that every inch of ground was to be held. Nevertheless these new orders were issued. They could not be carried out, because the situation deteriorated so rapidly and because the fighting effectiveness of the infantry divisions had been reduced by years of neglect.

After the fall of Cherbourg, the main effort of the American First Army centered in the St. Lô-Carentan area. The American divisions first tried to seize the Coutances-St. Lô line, so that they might have a more favorable line of departure for further operations. A battle of attrition, similar to that fought at Caen, was now started in the St. Lô area. The German ground troops, receiving no support from other army services, had to hold out without relief and without reinforcements.

Between July 1 and 24, the Allied Twenty-first Army Group tried to force a breakthrough both at Caen and at St. Lô.

The British Second Army moved out on July 8 to encircle Caen from the north and west with three of its infantry divisions and four or five armored brigades. During the previous night the whole area on both sides of the Orne River had been pulverized by artillery, naval gunfire, and saturation bombing. Most of the Panzer reserves of the Germans were knocked out and thrown like toys into the bomb craters. The British succeeded in taking Caen after two days of struggle, but a crossing of the Orne was prevented by throwing in our last reserves and by the brave self-sacrifice of the German troops. After their exertions in the battle for Caen, the British spent several days regrouping and preparing their forces. Radio silence and "smoke screens" made any ground reconnaissance on our part impossible; observation planes could not pierce their artificial fog banks. The German command lacked the information on which sound decisions could be made. British local attacks continued, but they were on a small scale and intended merely to improve the front here and there.

The British main offensive began on July 18, with the main effort east of the Orne. Several hours of artillery barrage, both light and heavy, more than a thousand fighter planes, and 2,200 bombers prepared the attack. The British threw in five infantry divisions, three armored divisions and three armored brigades—more than a thousand armored vehicles deployed along a very narrow front. During four days of violent battle they advanced about five miles, but the expected breakthrough did not succeed. The German Panzer grenadiers and infantry, despite their heavy losses and complete exhaustion, withstood this attack also and prevented a breakthrough.

The battle around Caen reached a climax on July 20, and at the last hour ended in success for the defensive forces.

Meanwhile, the inferior German Seventh Army fought against the American First Army on the Cotentin peninsula and at St. Lô. Here too the Allied tactics of wearing down resistance by a massed attack of all arms consumed the strength of the German divisions. Between July 3 and 7, four American divisions attempted to break through southward between the Prairie Marécageuse de Gorges (the marshlands of Gorges) and the west coast. They were able to advance about three miles and then were halted.

Fighting on the western side of the Cotentin peninsula was local in character, while the Americans concentrated their strength in the St. Lô area and between the Vire and the Taute. During the night of July 18-19, the enemy succeeded in encircling and capturing the ruins of St. Lô, which had been the headquarters of the LXXXIV Corps. The Corps Commander, General Erich Marcks, who had lost a leg in the Russian campaign, was killed close to the line of battle. After taking St. Lô, the enemy attack focused on the area west of the Vire and began a big offensive on July 24, following an unbelievably heavy artillery bombardment, in an attempt to smash the front between the Vire and the sea. Evidence that this attack would bring about a decisive breakthrough soon became apparent. The few reserves that could be sent in to stem the American attack came too late and in scattered groups.

East of St. Lô a breakthrough had barely been prevented on July 24; but west of that city it succeeded. The opportunity for freedom of maneuver beckoned the American First Army towards the interior of France.

By then the Allies had landed forty divisions, all armored or motorized, and more units were still landing.

The German Command expected that the British Second Army would continue its breakthrough attacks with its main force east of the Orne, in order to reach the Falaise area and use it for a jumping-off place. It was thought that the American First Army would widen and complete its breakthrough and push across the Domfront-Avranches line into the heart of France, and that some units of the

British Second Army would join the west flank of the American advance.

Wiping out the invasion forces in Normandy by means of offensive action, as Hitler had wished and ordered, was now unthinkable. It was questionable whether the already successfully invaded area could be sealed off.

The Commander in Chief of Army Group B reported as early as July 12 that the enemy had nearly achieved his objective of exhausting the strength of the German forces.

The ultimatum that Field Marshal Rommel sent to Hitler on July 15 will be discussed later.

THE POLITICAL EVENTS

The tactical and military developments up to July 24 have been dealt with first, because they form the foundation for an evaluation of the political events and changes in command that took place during this period of time.

During the days following the Margival conference, the Army Group Commander and his Chief of Staff informed the commanders of subordinate armies, several corps and divisional commanders, and their chiefs of staff regarding the outcome of the "discussion with the Führer" and the conclusions that might be drawn. Rommel told the commanders more or less frankly, depending on their political leanings, that in the course of ensuing military events independent action might have to be taken on the western front by the Wehrmacht. Colonel Generals von Salmuth, and Dollmann, and General Geyr von Schweppenburg agreed with Rommel's military and political evaluation of the situation, and expressed their confidence in him. They said that they were ready to carry out his orders, even if these were in contradiction to the orders of the Führer.

June 25 seemed a particularly significant day because of simultaneous military and political events and conferences.

The Soviet Army had broken through on the front of the Central Army Group along the Smolensk-Minsk highway. and was approaching the frontiers of the Reich. In Normandy the enemy attacked near Tilly with superior armored forces and made a breach in the line three miles long and three miles deep, which threatened to make Caen untenable.

That day an officer of the General Staff, Colonel Finckh, the new Quartermaster-General for the West, came on behalf of General Eduard Wagner, the Quartermaster-General, and reported on the preparations for the elimination of Hitler and on the planned overthrow of the regime, which was to save Germany. He told of the failure of earlier attempts on the life of Hitler and of the preparations for a new attempt which was to be made at Berchtesgaden. Finckh was asked to inform his superiors that Rommel, for well-known reasons, thought an attempt on the life of Hitler to be inexpedient and still believed that he should be arrested and tried by a German court. He told Colonel Finckh to urge General Wagner to co-ordinate the plans of the conspirators at the General Headquarters of the Army and those in Germany. He wanted to have a report on this matter as soon as possible. Too many people, in Rommel's opinion, were discussing this vital question separately.

He thought it was essential to fix a definite time well in advance so that the revolt could be carefully prepared and its success guaranteed. He intended to visit Hitler once more himself and put forward his demands in the form of an ultimatum.

The field commanders had a good deal to say. Lieutenant General Count Schwerin, commander of the 116th Panzer Division, submitted a memorandum on the military and political situation, demanding in the name of his troops that the war should be brought to a close and the National Socialist regime removed. He declared that his division was reliable and could be used against internal enemies. The same was true of the Second Panzer under Lieutenant General Baron von Lüttwitz.

Rundstedt and Rommel had often discussed and had agreed on the headlong deterioration of conditions not only on the western front but on all fronts. They urgently requested another conference with Hitler. Both field marshals were summoned to Berchtesgaden on June 28 on such short notice that they had to drive through part of the night to reach Upper Bavaria. Flying was forbidden. Although the field marshals reached Berchtesgaden in the late morning of June 29, they had to wait until evening before Hitler received them. The conference took place in the presence of a large group. The field marshals pressed Hitler to consider the rapidly deteriorating war situation and take steps to end hostilities. Hitler gave them no direct answer, but lapsed into a lengthy discourse about continuing the war with the aid of "miracle weapons." Just as the death of the empress of Russia had been the turning point for Frederick the Great in the Seven Years' War, he exclaimed, the new German weapons would produce "the miraculous turning point of the war." Their use would be the prelude to "final and total victory." His discourse became lost in fantastic digressions. The field marshals repeated their demand for a private interview with him, but it was refused. He did not even invite them to dinner, and curtly gave them leave to depart. Rommel therefore reiterated his views on the general situation to Field Marshal Keitel in these words:

"A total victory, to which Hitler is still referring even today, is absurd in our rapidly worsening situation, and a total defeat can be expected. Our aim should be to use every means to end the war in the west immediately, renouncing all that we have won up to now and abandoning all our wishful dreams, so that we can hold the eastern front. We must save Germany from chaos and especially from complete destruction by enemy bombing."

Keitel listened to his personal report and promised to present the situation to Hitler along these lines. At the end he declared resignedly, "I too am aware that there is nothing more to be done."

This declaration by Keitel seems particularly interesting because after July 20 he sat on the so-called Court of Honor of the German Wehrmacht, which condemned his old comrades and dismissed them from the service. On that occasion he seems to have given an entirely different picture of the situation.

The field marshals returned to their battle headquarters with their mission unfulfilled, wrapped in conflicting thoughts and tortured emotions.

The Seventh Army had lost its commander in the meantime. General Dollmann, who had worked day and night without sparing himself, succumbed to a heart attack early on June 29. He never learned that Hitler had demanded his recall. Rommel proposed as his successor one of the most eminent generals in the whole army, Erich Marcks, who was experienced in battle and immediately available. Hitler would not approve this choice for political reasons, because of a deep distrust of Marcks, once Director of the Cabinet Offices of General von Schleicher, who was murdered by order of the Nazi Party in 1934. Marcks was killed in battle three weeks later, as we have related.

Without further consultation with Rommel, SS Chief Group Leader Hausser, commander of the II SS Panzer Corps, was appointed to succeed Dollmann. Hausser had to leave his corps at the very moment when it was to lead the attack against the enemy front at Caen.

Hausser had served in the Army and the General Staff, but he had gone into the SS at an early date. He was soldierly, had drive and marked courage, but was difficult to fathom in political matters, a veritable Janus. His appointment was received with mixed feelings; he was younger in service than many commanding generals and, in particular, the commander of the Western Panzer Group.

Rundstedt was relieved of command of the western front two days after returning from the conference with the Führer, "for reasons of health." Hitler possessed neither the courage nor the tact to tell his oldest field marshal personally of his recall. Instead he sent his second adjutant, Lieutenant Colonel Borgmann, a member of the General Staff, to St. Germain, with a letter and the Oak Leaves for the Knight's Cross of the Iron Cross. Rundstedt made a farewell visit to Rommel at La Roche Guyon on July 4, and said that he was thankful that he would not be in command during the coming catastrophe. The next day the commander of the Western Panzer Group, General Geyr von Schweppenburg, was relieved of his command without previous notice. General Heinz Eberbach was appointed to replace him. The Panzer Group was renamed the Fifth Panzer Army.

General Baron von Schweppenburg was held responsible for the failure of the II SS Panzer Corps's counterattack. Hitler communicated his decision to him on the telephone and reproached him with growing defeatism. He had made a clear situation report after the collapse of the attack and had recommended that Caen and the area west of the Orne should be evacuated. He also demanded freedom of action and ended his report with the words:

"We must choose between tactical patchwork within a

strategy of rigid, unyielding defense, a strategy which yields complete initiative to the enemy, and a system of elastic tactics which at least partially preserves for us the initiative. The Panzer Group believes that the latter is the more correct and more forceful decision."

Rommel passed on this report verbatim, expressed his full agreement with it, and emphasized once more the demand for freedom of maneuver. When he heard of the recall of Geyr von Schweppenburg, he at once supported his group commander, but his protests were brusquely turned down by Keitel.

The new commander, General Eberbach, was an able soldier with a great deal of experience in armored warfare. His character, conduct, and political insight made him a particularly gifted leader of men.

Officers and troops alike expected that their experienced and battle-tried army group commander, Marshal Rommel, would succeed Rundstedt in the western command. To their surprise, the new Commander in Chief of Western Forces was Field Marshal Günther von Kluge. Hitler's mistrust of Rommel had already become too strong.

Günther von Kluge was an artillery officer who had held all positions in the General Staff. He had distinguished himself in the campaign of 1940 as commander of the Fourth Army. Under his command Rommel had led the "Phantom" division in its famous thrust to the coast. Kluge had proved himself a master of improvisation and tenacity as Supreme Commander of the Central Army Group on the Russian front. He was sober, energetic, quick of grasp, courageous and hard on himself, but inclined to pose. The troops nicknamed him the "klugen (cunning) Hans." He was remorseless in insisting on the last ounce of effort from his subordinates. The cold eyes in his sharply chiseled features concealed emotions that he would not admit. In his personal conversations he showed a strong love of nature and a great interest in military subjects and modern history. He did not accept Hitler, and yet felt himself bound to him; perhaps he was swayed by a sense of being obligated for the special honors and gifts he had accepted from Hitler.

He had recovered from an automobile accident in the winter of 1943–44, when his car had overturned on the Minsk-Smolensk highway. He gave the impression of freshness and elasticity. Kluge had just passed a fortnight in Berchtesgaden, where Hitler had instructed him on his new task and had convinced him that the disasters in the west were the result of bad leadership and the mistakes and omissions of the armies in the field.

There was a frosty encounter between the two field marshals when Kluge arrived at La Roche Guyon on the afternoon of July 5. During the discussion in the hall of arms of the chateau, Kluge stated that the recall of Field Marshal von Rundstedt was the outward sign of Hitler's dissatisfaction with the leadership in the West. Rommel himself did not enjoy the absolute confidence of the Führer. The impression at Supreme Headquarters was that now, as in Africa, Rommel was too easily influenced by the "allegedly overpowering effect of the enemy's weapons" and was too inclined to pessimism. Rommel was also daily displaying his obstinacy and was not carrying out the Führer's orders wholeheartedly.

"Field Marshal Rommel," Kluge concluded, "even you must obey unconditionally from now on. This is good advice that I am giving you."

This led to a vehement dispute between the two field marshals, during which Rommel repeatedly and insistently told Kluge to draw his own conclusions from the general situation and its requirements. Rommel in heightened tones protested against the unjustified criticisms of Hitler and the High Command. The conversation became so heated that Kluge ordered the Chief of Staff and the operations officers (1A) of the Army Group to leave the room.

Rommel demanded that the new Commander in Chief withdraw his accusations at once, and subsequently in writing, and so inform the High Command of the Armed Forces. Rommel set a time limit by which his demand was to be met. He advised Kluge not to form any opinions until he had conferred with his army commanders and with the troops and had made a tour of inspection at the front.

There was a strong feeling of resentment between them after this conference. Kluge did not go into the general situation, and Rommel was bitter that Kluge was not more inclined to discuss the burning question of how to save the Reich from destruction. Rommel had confidential information that had led him to the justified conclusion that Kluge had been in touch with opposition forces in Germany for years. Now he appeared as the mouthpiece of Hitler and had spoken in the Berchtesgaden style without any firsthand knowledge of conditions at the front.

Following an itinerary prepared by the Army Group, Kluge made a two-day tour of inspection beginning on July 6, and talked to all available commanders and troops. Saul was converted to Paul. The overwhelming evidence of the facts and the clarifying views of all the commanding officers made him realize that Rommel was right and that he had temporarily been blinded by Hitler's deceptive phrases.

He took back all his accusations, excusing his behavior on the grounds that Hitler and Keitel had given him false information. He observed that Hitler did not want to see the true situation in spite of all reports, telephone calls, and personal interviews. Hitler lived in a world of dreams and when the dreams faded looked around for scapegoats.

This had been the essence of Kluge's experience on the Russian front.

A lieutenant colonel of the reserves, Dr. von Hofacker, arrived at La Roche Guyon on July 9 under instructions from the Military Governor of France, General von Stülpnagel. Hofacker was a son of a Württemberg corps commander in Italy in World War I, under whom Rommel had earned his Pour le Mérite for storming Monte Matajur. Colonel von Hofacker was also a cousin of Colonel Count Klaus von Stauffenberg, a member of the General Staff, who had notified the Chief of Staff of Army Group B of his impending visit on behalf of General Beck. The events of July 20, however, made this visit impossible. Cäsar von Hofacker, a man of political talents, enthusiasm, and rare persuasiveness, had been an important figure in the German steel industry in Berlin before the war, and during recent years Stülpnagel's most trusted staff officer. He was accompanied by a confidant of Stülpnagel, Dr. Max Horst, and was supposed to form a final opinion on conditions at the front for Beck and Stauffenberg. He presented a well-written memorandum that embodied the views of the military governor. It urged quick and determined action in view of the military and political situation, and ended with an appeal by all resistance forces for the field marshal to take independent action at once to end the war in the west. It was an appeal for open rebellion and coincided with the view of the conspirators in Berlin that the Allies would never deal with Hitler or his cohorts, Göring, Himmler, or Ribbentrop. These must be done away with at the same time as the National Socialist system. The memorandum emphasized the point raised in earlier discussions by Rommel that the enemy bombing attacks should be stopped in order to give Germany moral and economic respite. Hofacker asked how long the German front in the west could be held. The Berlin decisions would be substantially influenced by the answer to this question. The answer Rommel gave was equally direct: "At the most fourteen days to three weeks. Then a breakthrough may be expected. We have no additional forces to throw into battle."

Hofacker was to report to Marshal von Kluge, and then go to Berlin to brief General Beck and other members of the resistance forces and synchronize the plans to overthrow the National Socialist state. He was to report to Rommel again after July 15.

The technical possibility of a local suspension of hostilities in order to cross the lines and negotiate with the enemy was tried out during these days by General Baron von Lüttwitz in the 2nd Panzer sector. The Allied command had offered by radio to exchange German female personnel of the medical and communications services captured in Cherbourg for severely wounded Allied soldiers, at a place designated by the Allies. During two hours of local armistice this humanitarian act took place. Hitler was furious and mistrustful when he heard about this.

Field Marshal von Kluge came back to La Roche Guyon on July 12. The marshals discussed tactical events and operations, and they reached complete agreement on the military problems. Kluge asked for a final estimate of how long the front could be held with the strength of the fighting units ebbing and no reserves behind them. Rommel agreed that the Army leaders and the majority of the corps commanders should be asked to give their opinions. He suggested that their answers be forwarded to Hitler together with an ultimatum. He revealed what he thought should be done, if as expected, Hitler rejected these demands. He told Kluge of the mission of Hofacker, who would soon return with news from Berlin. The Quartermaster General was to report within a few days on the situation at the Russian front and at Army headquarters.

Kluge listened attentively, then stated that he agreed in principle with Rommel's ideas and would make his final decision dependent on the reports that the field commanders would send. Rommel instructed his Chief of Staff to inform General von Stülpnagel of his intentions and of his conversations with Kluge. It was to be emphasized to Stülpnagel that Rommel was ready under any circumstances to take action even if Kluge could not decide to take part. General Speidel visited Stülpnagel in Paris late on July 13. The Military Governor had just received news of the arrest of Leuschner and Leber, Social Democrat leaders of the resistance forces, in Berlin. It seemed that there was need for quick action. Stülpnagel proposed that nothing should be done until Hofacker returned. The Military Governor had completed all preparations for the *coup d'état* within the area of his command.

Field Marshal Rommel went to the front on July 13, 14, and 15, and held discussions with all his commanders, including the SS Commanders, Sepp Dietrich and Hausser, whose reports on the situation at the front sounded particularly serious. They were absolutely frank, and Rommel did not anticipate any difficulties with his SS troops if he decided to act independently in the west. The commanding general of the I SS Panzer Corps and later commander of the Fifth Panzer Army, SS Chief Group Leader Dietrich, had expressed disagreement with the leadership of the Führer to both Rommel and his Chief of Staff during a visit to La Roche Guyon. He too demanded "independent action if the front is broken." The SS units engaged in battle against the enemy and fighting bravely were firmly controlled by their commander. It should be said in justice to the SS fighting units that they completely disassociated

6. SURRENDER AT CHERBOURG

themselves from the secret police portions of their own SS and their methods of operation.

The Military Governor thought that in case of need he could eliminate the Security Service in France and in Paris without much trouble.

Rommel came back from the front deeply thoughtful and moved. He had talked with the front-line troops and they had complemented and confirmed the picture that the army commanders and commanding generals had drawn. Everywhere he was confronted with the anxious question whether drastic and independent action by the high commanders might not alter the situation at the last hour. The Field Marshal gave explanations where it seemed appropriate and came back with the heartening assurance that the troops and officers of all ranks had full confidence in *his* leadership.

All other possibilties of bringing the truth home to Hitler had been exhausted. Instead of the military assistance promised by Hitler there had been petty sulking and malevolent suspicion. Amateurish orders from Bavaria and East Prussia continued to accumulate. Once more Rommel sent a message to Hitler, but this time in the form of an unmistakably severe ultimatum. It was sent to Hitler on July 15 in a three-page memorandum on the military teletype via the Commander in Chief for the West. Its text was approximately as follows:

The position in Normandy becomes more difficult from day to day. A grave crisis is at hand.

Because of the severity of the battle, the extraordinary amount of matériel thrown in by the enemy, particularly in artillery and armor, and the effect of his air force, which dominates the battle area unopposed, our losses are so high that the fighting strength of our divisions is dwindling fast.

Replacements from Germany are sparse and transport difficulties prevent them from reaching the front for weeks. There have been only 6,000 replacements as compared with the loss of 97,000 men, of whom 2,360 were officers (28 generals and 354 officers of field rank)—an average of 2,500 to 3,000 casualties a day. The matériel losses in the field have been extremely high, and it has not been possible to replace more than a small part of them. There have been 225 tanks destroyed and only 17 replacements received. The newly arrived divisions are inexperienced in battle, lack artillery, armor-piercing weapons and close-range antitank weapons. They are not capable of successfully withstanding heavy attacks after hours of artillery and aerial bombardment. As has been proved in battles, even the bravest troops are smashed to pieces under the weight of such attacks.

The supply situation is made so difficult by the destruction of the railway system and the bombing of the highways and roads up to 100 miles behind the front that only the most vital necessities can be brought up. Artillery and mortar ammunition has to be used most sparingly.

There are no reinforcements of any importance that can be brought to the Normandy front. Day after day new forces are landed by the enemy, and masses of war matériel are brought ashore. Our air forces do not disturb the enemy supply lines. Enemy pressure is continually increasing.

It must therefore be expected that the Allies will succeed within a short time—fourteen days to three weeks—in breaking through our weak lines, particularly on the Seventh Army front, and will push far on into the interior of France. The consequences are not foreseeable.

The troops are fighting heroically everywhere, but the unequal struggle is nearing its end.

The Field Marshal terminated with a postscript in his own handwriting: "I must beg you to draw the political conclusions without delay. I feel it my duty as the Commander

in Chief of the Army Group to state this clearly . . .
Rommel, Field Marshal."

The word "political" was omitted when the message was
relayed, so that the word "conclusions" could be made to
include both military and political matters.

The word "political" would have been like waving a red
cloth before Hitler and would have produced aimless rages
instead of sensible reflection, and the troops would have
been subjected to some senseless new order given in anger.
Field Marshal von Kluge, in forwarding it, stated that he
agreed with the opinions and demands of Rommel. (The
original copy of this telegram, with Rommel's postscript
and marginal notations, had to be destroyed later on, when
the Chief of Staff of Army Group B was arrested.)

The Marshal had raised his voice in warning for the last
time. He said after sending the ultimatum: "I have given
him his last chance. If he does not take it, we will act."

The fair towns of Germany, the homeland that he loved,
were still largely undamaged by the war. The major part
of the German provinces was still untouched by the storm.
Needless sacrifices that nobody could justify, the deaths
of many thousands of all nations, the horror of the death
struggle on the soil of Germany, were still avoidable.

Erwin Rommel was quite clear as to the final consequences of his decision to act independently and had no
illusions about the conditions of the peace. They would
be unsparing and hard. He hoped for a measure of statesmanlike insight, psychological wisdom, and political planning in the Allied deliberations. He expected no sympathy
or any kindred emotion, but he relied on the calculated understanding of the great powers.

Rommel spoke of these matters late in the evening of
July 15 with Vice-Admiral Ruge and the Chief of Staff.

On that evening he was sustained by a comforting feeling of confidence, as he seldom had been during these weeks of heavy burden. He sought and found its confirmation in looking up at the eternal stars.

But in the days that followed, all those who shared his thoughts were to see that an inscrutable higher power, in the hollow of whose hand lay the destiny of man, was pursuing its own course. There was to be no act of liberation.

The crisis in the Caen area was mounting from hour to hour, deep thrusts by the enemy were sealed off with difficulty and with heroic sacrifice. The decisive breakthrough of the Allies toward Paris was imminent.

The Field Marshal drove to a danger spot on the front early on July 17, to take charge of the situation himself, restore order, and encourage the exhausted troops. He singled out some commanding officers and told them of his demands to Hitler and what he expected next. On the basis of a call from his Chief of Staff, he decided to return earlier than he had at first intended. But a local crisis in the battle made his presence necessary. He drove to the headquarters of the I SS Panzer Corps and visited Sepp Dietrich. He left there at 4:00 P.M. to return to La Roche Guyon. On the road between Livarot and Vimoutiers, near an estate named Montgomery, enemy fighter aircraft caught sight of the staff car, which as always was unaccompanied. They had no idea that they were in pursuit of the best man on the western front, the one who embodied the only hope that Germany had of salvation. Just before the car reached the protective cover of a grove of poplars, three of the fighters dived on the car, spraying it with bursts of fire. The driver was killed, and the Field Marshal was wounded so severely that he was at first thought dead.

Rommel was in fact eliminated in the very hour that his army and his people could spare him least. All those who were groping with his help to find a way to a new and better world felt themselves painfully deprived of their pillar of strength.

Ernst Jünger wrote of this moment:

The blow that felled Rommel on the Livarot road on July 17, 1944, deprived our plan of the only man strong enough to bear the terrible weight of war and civil war simultaneously, the only man who was straightforward enough to counter the frightful folly of the leaders of Germany. This was an omen which had only one interpretation.

And so it was.

Field Marshal von Kluge
Takes Over Command
of Army Group B

THE PLOT OF JULY 20, 1944

AT FIRST the Army Group remained leaderless. Hitler's chief adjutant, General Schmundt, suggested as a successor to Rommel SS Chief Group Leader Hausser, who had taken command of the Seventh Army only three weeks before, with Sepp Dietrich to take over Hausser's command. It was obvious that the "Praetorian Guard" were beginning to assume command everywhere on the western front. Field Marshal von Kluge turned down this proposal firmly, and on the evening of July 19 took over command of the Army Group himself, without relinquishing the western command. He moved into La Roche Guyon, leaving at western headquarters in St. Germain his Chief of Staff, General Blumentritt, who was to deal with all matters that did not concern Army Group B.

Early on the morning of July 20, Marshal von Kluge

drove to the Fifth Panzer Army headquarters, where he had ordered that all his army and corps commanders meet him. He gave them instructions concerning the battle in the critical Caen and St. Lô areas. Political matters were not brought up at all.

General Blumentritt and Colonel Finckh telephoned the Chief of Staff of Army Group B at 5:00 P.M. on July 20, and informed him: "Hitler is dead."

But when Kluge returned an hour or two later the radio already announced that the attempt on the life of Hitler had failed. This was confirmed by telephone calls from Hitler's headquarters, which gave details of what had happened.

Field Marshal Sperrle, General von Stülpnagel, and General Blumentritt arrived at La Roche Guyon between 7:00 and 8:00 P.M. Stülpnagel and Lieutenant Colonel von Hofacker pleaded with Kluge to take part in these momentous events. Although the attempt on the life of Hitler had failed, the Army Headquarters in Berlin was still in the hands of the rebels, under control of the military leader of the conspiracy, General Beck. They urged that only by immediately ending the war, even if it meant capitulation, thereby presenting a *fait accompli*, would it be possible to give the otherwise abortive uprising in Berlin a chance of success.

General von Stülpnagel, on leaving Paris, had ordered the commandant of the city, Baron von Boineburg, to arrest the senior SS chief and police chief of France, Chief Group Leader Oberg, together with his staff and the entire Secret Police, some 1,200 SS officials. Security units of the army under the command of Colonel von Kraewel carried out these arrests without a shot being fired. It was explained to the troops that Hitler had been killed by SS units and that there was a danger that the SS might assume tyrannical power.

Field Marshal von Kluge telephoned personally to Colonel Generals Beck, Fromm, and Höppner, and to Generals Warlimont and Stieff, but he could not decide to assume leadership of an uprising on the western front. Kluge did not believe that isolated action could be taken in the west if the revolt in Berlin and the plot in the Führer's headquarters had failed. Above all he was not sure that he could rely on his officers and troops in this new situation.

Kluge telephoned again to the Führer's headquarters and to the Army Headquarters in Berlin. Then he ordered the Military Governor of France to release the imprisoned Secret Police. The fate of General von Stülpnagel was thus sealed. Stülpnagel passed on these orders by telephone to his Chief of Staff, Colonel von Linstow, at his headquarters, where Admiral Krancke, naval commander in the west, Ambassador Abetz, and others, full of alarm, had already arrived.

During these ominous evening hours of July 20, a crisis had arisen on the front at Caen and St. Lô. Corps commanders and division commanders telephoned the Army Group Headquarters, calling for reserves and asking for news of the events in Hitler's headquarters and in Berlin, about which they had heard on the radio. The Chief of Staff of Army Group B had to answer these questions himself and alone take the necessary measures to hold the front.

The field marshal invited General von Stülpnagel, Lieutenant Colonel von Hofacker, and Dr. Horst to have supper with him. They ate in silence by candlelight, as if they sat in a house just visited by death. Those who survived never forgot the ghostly atmosphere of this hour. General von Stülpnagel returned that night to Paris and was relieved of his command immediately, being replaced by General Blumentritt. Field Marshal Keitel spoke to Stülpnagel on the telephone, ordering him to return to Berlin and report. He left Paris early on July 21 without informing von Kluge. Near Verdun, where he fought in the first World War, he tried to take his life with a pistol. The shot blinded him and he was taken to Verdun Military Hospital, where he was treated as a Gestapo prisoner.

As he regained consciousness after an operation, he cried out the name "Rommel!" Before he had fully recovered from his wound, he was dragged to Berlin, tried by the People's Court, and condemned to death by hanging. He was hanged on August 30, along with the colonels of the General Staff, von Listow and Finckh. Lieutenant Colonel von Hofacker suffered the same fate on December 20. The Chief of Staff of Army Group B, himself a prisoner, saw him in the Gestapo cellars in Prinz Albrechtstrasse for the last time on December 19, still unbowed.

Field Marshal von Kluge had first received the political leader of the unlucky conspiracy, Lord Mayor Dr. Goerdeler, in April 1942 at the Smolensk headquarters of the Central Army Group. He subsequently had exchanged views with General Beck, Ambassador von Hassell, and others. Kluge is supposed to have declared in 1943 that he was willing to help overthrow the National Socialist regime in Germany on two conditions: Hitler must be dead and Kluge must have supreme command of one of the two fronts, east or west. As of July 4, one of these conditions had been met, but the other, the decisive condition, was not fulfilled.

Major General Henning von Tresckow, who had been Kluge's operations officer (1A) for many years in the Central Army Group, was to have accompanied his commander in chief to the western front as chief of staff; in fact, Hitler's chief adjutant, Lieutenant General Schmundt, had unwittingly helped to further this move. But Kluge did not accept this proposal, probably because he feared Tresckow's inflexible will and desire for revolution that had drawn him daily into the dangers of conspiracy while they were together on the Russian front. So Tresckow, one of the most passionate and upright fighters against Hitler, a man of superlative character and mind, remained on the eastern front as Chief of Staff of the Second Army, and took his own life on July 21 to escape the hangman. In his testament Tresckow said: "Now the whole world will turn against us and revile us. But my conviction that we have done right is still as firm as ever. I consider Hitler to be not only the arch enemy of Germany but the arch enemy of the world. When I appear a few hours from now before the Throne of God to render account for my deeds and omissions, I believe I will be able to answer with good conscience for all that I have done in the struggle against Hitler. As God told Abraham that he would not destroy Sodom if only ten righteous men were to be found in the city, it is my hope that, for our sake, God will not destroy Germany. None of us can complain of our death. Those who joined our company put on the shirt of Nessus. The moral worth of a man begins at that moment when he is willing to sacrifice his life for his convictions."

Kluge had received a visit from Colonel von Böselager just before taking up the command of the western front. The colonel, who was killed in battle at the front shortly afterwards, conveyed to Kluge an appeal from Tresckow to take action on the basis of their previous conversations.

The bomb attempt on the life of Hitler on July 20 completely surprised von Kluge. The Quartermaster General, General Wagner, and Colonel von Stauffenberg, of the General Staff, had not visited him as expected, and he had no knowledge of the reasons that prevented them from coming.

Von Hofacker had been on the way back from Berlin on July 17, when he heard at the station that Rommel had been severely wounded. It was not possible to inform Kluge that an attempt on the life of Hitler was imminent, because the final decision to act on July 20 was taken in Berlin only on the afternoon of July 19.

The commissar-like political officer attached to Western Command Headquarters appeared on the morning of July 21 at La Roche Guyon with representatives of the Propaganda Department for France. They had been sent by Goebbels and Keitel, and demanded that a telegram of allegiance be sent to Hitler by Kluge, the text of which they had already prepared. They demanded moreover that he should broadcast on all German radio stations. Kluge was able to avoid making the broadcast, but he had to sign a modified version of the "congratulatory telegram."

Nevertheless, Günther von Kluge was to be drawn into the whirlpool of July 20. Fate does not spare the man whose convictions are not matched by his readiness to give them effect. After July 20 Kluge was increasingly distrusted by Hitler and the High Command of the Armed Forces, probably because of confessions forced from some of the prisoners. From then on his command activities were severely criticized and even sabotaged by orders from Obersalzberg.

Dr. Ley, leader of the Labor Front, made a ranting speech on the air, directed against the officer corps and the German aristocracy. Three of the divisional commanders of Army Group B—Baron von Funk, Baron von Lüttwitz, and Count von Schwerin—protested against this speech and demanded that Ley withdraw his accusations. SS Chief

Group Leader Sepp Dietrich made himself their spokes-man.

The new Chief of the German General Staff, Colonel General Heinz Guderian, issued an Order of the Day implicating the General Staff in the preparation and execution of the assassination plot of July 20. The Chief of Staff of Army Group B, with the assent of Marshal von Kluge, did not pass along this order to subordinate commanders. The Hitler salute or "Sieg Heil" was introduced at a time when every soldier suspected the imminent collapse of the system which demanded this token of allegiance. This seemed a satanical farce.

3

The Period from July 25 to August 18

AVRANCHES-MORTAIN

AND

THE BATTLE OF THE FALAISE POCKET

THERE WAS something almost ironical in the July 24 directive from the High Command of the Wehrmacht. It indicated that the attempt to prevent an American breakthrough on the Cotentin peninsula would be decisive for the whole western campaign, but it was combined with the order that still prohibited German field commanders freedom of maneuver.

General Patton, the aggressive and temperamental commander of the American Third Army, who had just landed on the Cotentin peninsula while the German High Command was still expecting him to land elsewhere, was pushing ruthlessly into the interior of France. This made it all the more necessary for the German Command to make drastic strategic decisions. With the lack of any reserves, and especially air forces, such orders as "hold every foot of ground under all circumstances and prevent the enemy from breaking through" were empty phrases.

The weight of the offensive of the two American armies had now been shifted to the western flank. Here a break-through to the south and southeast, cutting off the Breton peninsula, was to be expected within a few days. This would not only threaten to encircle from the west the Seventh Army and the Fifth Panzer Army in Normandy, it also was to develop into a decisive attack towards the Paris area and, beyond that, into Germany itself—it was the beginning of the end. Only over-all and large-scale meas-ures could be of any use now—such as the abandonment of the Mediterranean front, the withdrawal north of the whole Army Group G, the creation of strategic reserves at the expense of the individual armies and the organization of a rearward defense line along the Seine.

Neither Hitler nor the High Command could be per-suaded to make any decision.

The first danger that Marshal von Kluge foresaw when news came of the American breakthrough at St. Lô was that the Seventh Army would lose the protection that the Gulf of St. Malo afforded on its western flank. He then designated Avranches as the key point that must be held until countermeasures could be taken or entirely new or-ders received from the High Command. His foresight was proved correct. He knew that he could ask no more of the German troops. They had been in gruelling defensive battle for seven weeks, exposed to the destructive power of the Allied air forces, which had worked closely with the American ground forces to achieve the breakthrough at St. Lô.

All the reserves of the Seventh Army had been brought to the Cotentin front, but the antitank forces promised by the German High Command did not materialize. The High

Command would not even agree to the proposal to bring up the five divisions of the XXV Corps from the Breton peninsula. The front between Caen and St. Lô had been stripped to a practically insupportable extent. The bow was overstretched, the High Command did nothing, and the west was lost.

The XXXXVII Panzer Corps, consisting of the 2nd and 116th divisions, was to be assembled in the area west of the Vire to strike at the flank of the enemy forces which had broken through.

The Seventh Army, in the meantime, had taken the independent decision to move those forces of its own west flank that had been cut off by the breakthrough at St. Lô southeastward and to unite with the XXXXVII Panzer Corps, which was assembling for counterattack. On July 29 Field Marshal von Kluge countermanded the Seventh Army's order, because it meant relinquishing Avranches without a struggle. The counter orders came too late. The American armored divisions and air forces were surging forward too fast. Patton's armored forces occupied Avranches on July 30-31. The final breakthrough was within the enemy's grasp; the crisis had reached its peak. The German front between St. Lô and the Bay of St. Malo had been torn apart. Isolated groups of fighting men, bravely led, held out like breakwaters which would inevitably be overwhelmed in a matter of days or even hours. Kluge telephoned to General Jodl at the High Command, explained this turning point, and requested an immediate audience with Hitler. He reminded Jodl of the sudden change of fortune of the French Army in the Battle of the Marne in 1914. In vain! Instead of taking a new over-all or strategic decision, Hitler sent the following order to Army Group B on August 1, 1944:

The enemy is not under any circumstances to be permitted to break out into the open. Army Group B will prepare a counterattack, using all Panzer units, to push through as far as Avranches, cut off the enemy units that have broken through and destroy them. All available Panzer forces are to be withdrawn from their present front sectors, even if there are no divisions to relieve them, and are to be employed for this purpose under the commanding general of the Panzer troops, Eberbach. The outcome of the campaign in France depends upon this counterattack.

Kluge immediately protested against this order, which would bring about the collapse of the whole front from the Orne to the area south of St. Lô and hasten the catastrophe. He demanded that his views be immediately transmitted to Hitler. Hitler replied that he insisted on the carrying out of his order. Kluge did his duty by pointing out again that he expected dire consequences: undoubtedly the front in Normandy opposite the British Second Army would collapse if the Panzer units which formed the backbone of the German defense were to be withdrawn. He proposed new strategic measures, above all that the German forces be withdrawn behind a Seine defense line and that southern and central France be abandoned. The German High Command flatly turned down the ideas of Army Group B and in the presence of the Chief of Staff spoke in the style of their master about "destroying the enemy in Normandy with the planned Panzer counterattack" and of the "certain final victory."

The Group that was to attack under the command of General Eberbach consisted of the XXXXVII Panzer Corps (2nd and 116th Panzer divisions) and the I SS Panzer Corps (1st and 2nd SS Panzer divisions). The II SS Panzer Corps (9th and 10th SS Panzer divisions) was to have been included, but the time factor and the situation made this impossible. Continuous Allied air attacks on the Panzer forces forced the postponement of the date of this attack again and again.

It was the evening of August 6 before the Panzer forces were assembled under unimaginable difficulties in the area east of Mortain. The counteroffensive began shortly after midnight, before the Allied air forces could resume their annihilating operations. Kluge himself rushed to the local command post. The attack was successful until dawn broke. The 2nd Panzer Division penetrated six miles into the Allied line, overrunning a considerable number of American armored units annd other troops. With the first daylight the Allied battle squadrons roared overhead in quick successive waves and smothered all movement. Three hundred German fighters had been assembled from all areas to give air cover for this attack; but not one of them appeared over the German units spearheading the attack. They had been involved in air battles as they took off and were destroyed. Thus it was possible for the Allied air forces alone to wreck this Panzer operation with the help of a well-co-ordinated ground-to-air communications system. The much weakened Panzer divisions reached their field bases again on the evening of August 7 after having sustained heavy losses. Hitler ordered that the attack be resumed on August 8. This attack was carried out principally by the 1st SS Panzer Division and was repulsed with heavy losses by American armored and air forces.

Had there been sufficient air support the counterattack might have broken through to its objective of Avranches some 15 miles away and would have won some time for strategic decisions, although it was unlikely, considering Hitler's mentality, that any such decision would have been made. How little he realized the true situation is evident from one of his orders on August 7 or 8 to "roll back the

Allied invasion front from the west eastward, following the attack by Eberbach's groups."

Portions of the American forces had nearly sealed off the Breton peninsula by August 5. The commanding general of the XXV Army Corps, General Farmbacher, stationed in Rennes, was therefore made commander of Brittany. He too was ordered "to hold off the enemy with all your strength," then fight back to the "fortresses" and "defend them to the last man." Shades of Cherbourg!

As a result the XXV Corps with its divisions was cut off and could play no part in subsequent events, not even to the extent of tying down enemy forces.

The counteroffensive having failed, Kluge requested again that southern France be relinquished and suggested that Army Group G be immediately withdrawn to the Seine-Loing line and then, along the Loire from Gien over Nevers to the Swiss frontier at Gex. Orders had been given in mid-July to survey the lower Seine and prepare defenses. The High Command postponed a decision.

The counteroffensive ordered by Hitler in the Mortain-Avranches area tied down the German Panzer forces south of the Seine and wasted them. This order was contrary to the laws of strategy as well as to common sense. It was an unexpected gift of decisive value to the enemy.

On August 9 and 10, General Patton gave an example of dashing armored leadership when the American Third Army pushed past Laval and the Alençon-Le Mans line in the direction of Paris. The 9th Panzer Division, thrown in south of Alençon in spite of the express orders of Hitler, managed to slow up the tempestous advance eastward and tied down some of the American forces. Now it became clear to all how disastrous had been the decision to leave the corps in Brittany where it was now battling to no purpose at all. More American forces came up in a steady stream, superior to the Germans in weapons and mobility.

Army Group B reported that the enemy probably intended to surround the Fifth Panzer and the Seventh armies west of the lower Seine, and demanded that these armies should be withdrawn and positions taken across the Seine and that Army Group G be withdrawn in conjunction with these two armies in order to prolong their defensive line to the east.

Hitler did not agree with the estimate of enemy strength submitted by von Kluge. The High Command would admit only the existence of "enemy armored spearheads" which could be disposed of by "improvised commando units."

Hitler still hesitated, then demanded that the battered Panzer group of Eberbach repeat its attack toward the coast. This was made impossible by the over-all situation and by the weakness of the Panzer groups.

On August 10, Field Marshal von Kluge made a suggestion that was intended to distract the attention of Hitler from a repetition of that senseless attack, and to gain time. He suggested to the High Command, "subject to future developments of the situation," that Eberbach's Panzer group should attack southward "to free the southern flank." When Kluge realized that this push would also have come too late, he ordered on his own initiative that the Fifth Panzer Army should withdraw steadily behind the Orne and then behind the Toucques sector, with the Seventh Army covering its Domfront-Alençon line and the eastern flank. Hitler agreed grudgingly on August 12 and made no further decision. Army Group G with its First and Nineteenth armies remained immobile—the former in the Bay of Biscay region and the latter along the Mediterranean coast.

Marshal von Kluge had lost his resiliency since the events

of July 20 and seemed at times to face the prospect of the inevitable collapse with fatalistic resignation. He tortured himself with thoughts of trying to find a way out of the dilemma after having failed to act against Hitler on July 20. But although he was repeatedly urged to do so, he could not quite decide to withdraw Army Group G on his own responsibility, and to give up the front south of the Seine and carry out a new strategy which would use his remaining forces wisely.

Strong Allied formations swept in a wide circling movement around the Domfront-Alençon line northward in the direction of Falaise, in order to surround the two German armies in Normandy, while others pushed on in the direction of Paris. On August 12 Kluge drove to the area south of Falaise to confer with the army and corps commanders. The mobile signal unit accompanying him was knocked out by a direct hit, and contact with the Commander in Chief was cut off. General Jodl telephoned the Chief of Staff of Army Group B and asked him repeatedly on behalf of Hitler whether he thought it possible that Marshal von Kluge had gone over to the enemy. When the field marshal returned, there was a teletype message from Hitler waiting for him: "Field Marshal von Kluge is to leave the Falaise pocket and direct the Normandy battle from the headquarters of the Fifth Panzer Army."

This militarily absurd command was evidence of the suspicion and nervousness of the Führer. Officers and men had already lost confidence in Hitler after the many contradictory orders they had received. They sensed in them Hitler's insecurity. Even if Kluge had not been able to command the whole front from the Falaise pocket, his presence there meant a great deal to the troops and he would have been able in case of need to give permission to his generals to break out eastward across the Seine.

On August 3 when the staff of the First Army was moved
from the Biscay area northward to take over command of
the "front" between the southeast wing of the Seventh
Army and the Loire, at Orléans, there were only service
and administrative personnel available to patch up a front.
Two divisions of the Fifteenth Army and two SS training brigades were to be brought up later. That same day
the first reports arrived of Allied troops embarking in Al-
giers: the Mediterranean coast of France was about to be
invaded. Even now Hitler and the High Command refused to move the nine divisions of Army Group G, which,
to be sure, had only a reduced fighting potential because
they lacked mobility. Hitler and the High Command did
not want to believe that a Mediterranean landing would
take place and that there was any connection between it
and the Allied operations between the Seine and the Loire.

Field Marshal von Kluge held a conference on August
14 in St. Germain to discuss the defense of Paris. He
brought together the commander in chief of the western
naval forces, the commander of the Third Air Fleet, the
new Military Governor of France, Air General Kitzinger,
and the newly appointed "Commandant of Greater
Paris," Infantry General von Choltitz. Hitler had ordered
that the city was to be defended to the last man and the
sixty-eight bridges of the Seine were to be blown up, as
well as all monuments and buildings of military importance.
The conference organized the evacuation of the armed
forces, together with their equipment and administrative
personnel, which was accomplished without difficulty. The
numerous party and state organizations quartered in Paris
departed in greater disorder. They had been set up in the
city independently of the military governor, and their
conduct often added no honor to the German name.

There were no combat troops available to defend the

populous capital. There were only security and reconnaissance units. It was obvious, moreover, to anyone with
common sense that the problems of supply would make it
impossible to hold Paris any length of time. For the same
realistic and idealistic reasons the French had surrendered
it in 1940.

In the meantime the Americans were increasing their
concentric pressure, mostly from the south and west
against the Trun-Argentan-Putanges front, while the British stood motionless. The German Panzer formations in the
Falaise pocket were holding open a corridor toward the
east. Instead of new strategic plans or assistance of any
kind, there arrived on August 15 an order bearing Hitler's
signature, which attempted to shift to von Kluge the blame
for the Allied breakthrough at Avranches, as well as the
failure of Eberbach's armored counterattack. This was one
of Hitler's typical "orders of the day" that had no military
value but would be useful for the "writing of history."

This order of the day arrived on the very day that the
Allies landed on the Côte d'Azur near Tropez, Cannes, and
St. Raphael. Hitler's estimate of the situation was proved
incorrect; the weak Mediterranean front collapsed. The
High Command was unwilling to order a withdrawal until
August 17, when it gave Army Group G permission to fall
back on the Orléans-Bourges-Montpellier line. This had
become impossible, as the Allied armored spearheads had
penetrated deeply from both invasion fronts and had in part
overtaken the German forces. Orders were also given to
hold the so-called southern "fortresses," namely, the northern and southern banks of the estuary of the Loire and the
city of La Rochelle.

Army Group B had renewed its request to permit the
Fifth Panzer and Seventh armies to break out of the ever-
shrinking Falaise pocket. When on August 15 Hitler pro-

hibited this move, Field Marshal von Kluge decided to order the retreat himself.

Without prior notification from the High Command, Field Marshal Model arrived at La Roche Guyon on the afternoon of August 16. He had been in command of the Central Army Group in the east after the whole front in Russia had collapsed on June 20 and been forced to withdraw as far as East Prussia. Hitler, in appointing him to his new command, had decorated him with the Diamonds of the Knight's Iron Cross. He handed Kluge a personal letter from Hitler explaining that he had decided to appoint Field Marshal Model commander in chief of the western front and of Army Group B because he had the impression that Kluge, after weeks of strain, was no longer physically able to carry out the duties of his command.

Von Kluge encountered Model with dignified bearing and, as he turned over the command to him, made it clear who was responsible for the deficiencies in command.

He said that his only regret was to have to leave his soldiers shedding their blood needlessly in the Falaise pocket at the orders of Hitler; he would feel close to them until his dying breath.

Marshal von Kluge was visibly moved as he said good-by to his small staff and left La Roche Guyon on August 18 at 5:00 P.M. Spearheads of the American First Army were already shelling the chateau with artillery and mortar fire. Between Verdun and Metz the field marshal of his own free will took a fatal dose of poison. His fate would have been an exemplary trial and the death by hanging that Hitler reserved for his field marshals and generals. His son and his son-in-law were taken into custody in accordance with the principle of "family responsibility."

Marshal von Kluge left behind a letter dated August 18, in which he summarized for Hitler the reasons that had

inevitably led to the collapse of the German front in Normandy. He said among other things that it would have been
impossible to prevent the breakthrough at Avranches in
the face of the enemy's superiority, after his proposed
strategy had been rejected and the promised reinforcements had failed to arrive. The counterattack at Mortain
ordered by Hitler against his advice had a decidedly adverse effect on the position of the Army Group.

Kluge ended his letter to Hitler with these words: "If
your new weapons have no effect, particularly in the air,
you must end the war. . . . The German people have suffered so unspeakably that it is high time to make an end
to this horror."

4

The Period from August 19 to September 5

WITHDRAWAL FROM THE FALAISE POCKET
TO THE WESTWALL

THE NEW Commander in Chief for the West and Commander of Army Group B, Field Marshal Model, had begun his military career as an infantry officer and at an early stage had been assigned to the General Staff. He had begun World War II as Chief of Staff of the Sixteenth Army on the western front, and had made a name for himself in the bitter winter warfare of 1941–42 in Russia as corps commander, then as commanding general of the Ninth Army. He showed determination, combined with a gift for improvisation. He was promoted in 1944 to command of the Central Army Group and remained there until he was assigned to the western command. Model was stocky, without social graces, extraordinarily active mentally and physically. He hardly knew what sleep was, and was not afraid to visit the front during the heat of battle. But his keen tactical sense was not balanced by an ability to judge what was possible. He overestimated his own ability, was erratic, and lacked a sense of moderation. He was inclined to curry favor with the troops at the expense of the officers. He was a one-sided soldier, inelegant and decidedly original in his mannerisms and conversation. Ardent by nature, he had often dared fate and he believed that his skill at improvisation and his good luck would bring him success in the west too. Although he had been schooled in strategy, he could not free himself of the details of tactical leadership. The saying "minima non curat praetor [the general doesn't attend to small details]" was unknown to Model. His unbalanced nature had made him submissive to the ideology of Hitler, although he often knew better.

He began his work, just as von Kluge had done on July 5, with preconceived notions and accusations against his new staff and the army commanders. The first orders that he gave were for continued resistance south of the Seine in the Falaise pocket; that is, they embodied the unimaginative idea that every inch of ground must be defended without hope of relief or even escape. Only when this became impossible would he permit the Somme-Marne line to be manned, and it was then to be held "under all circumstances." But there were no fortified positions on that line, nor had it even been reconnoitered.

The rapidly developing situation, which was like an avalanche, could not be stemmed in this way. Model did not want to make strategic decisions even when the need for them became urgently apparent. He followed the example and instructions of the German High Command.

After his initial sizing up of the situation on the western front, he demanded in writing thirty divisions and 200,000 men as replacements. He must have been well aware that this naive request could not be fulfilled; for when he was in command of the Central Army Group in Russia, which sustained such heavy losses after June 20, and when he reported to Hitler for new assignment, he had been informed concerning the numerical strength and condition of the High Command reserves.

The headquarters of Army Group B had to be evacuated from La Roche Guyon on August 18 under mortar and artillery fire of the American First Army, and moved to "the Führer's battle headquarters" at Margival, north of Soissons.

The same day Hitler authorized the withdrawal of Army Group G behind the line—the Marne-Saone-Swiss border. As usual it was too late. He indicated that Marseilles and Toulon were to be held as "fortresses" and were to receive additional troops and matériel. The LXIV Corps, stationed at the Bay of Biscay, was to be brought straight across central France in separate columns of march to join with Army Group G. It was easy for the American formations to harass these slow-moving German troops, overtaking them, splitting them up, and driving them northward.

In the meantime the Falaise pocket had narrowed daily; the American pressure from the west, south, and southeast surpassed that of the British.

Two army commands, four corps commands, nine infantry divisions, and about five Panzer divisions were being pressed together in a square about six to ten miles in size between Falaise and Argentan, under converging artillery fire of all calibers and exposed day and night to continuous bombing. The enemy air forces prevented supplies, especially fuel, from being brought up. However, the local army commanders did not lose their nerve and began on August 19–20 to carry out the confidential instructions that Marshal von Kluge had given them, pushing northwestward with the II SS Panzer Corps gallantly covering the retreat and absorbing the enemy pressure. It was a miracle that some of these formations managed to break out of the steel ring around them. They fell back in the direction of Rouen and held off the enemy, although they could only do so after heavy casualties and the loss of the bulk of their heavy equipment.

Meanwhile the American First Army had begun a wide encircling movement between Dreux and Paris. Advance guards had actually crossed the river between Vernon and Nantes. It was fortunate for the Germans that the American command did not exploit this river crossing.

A push along the north bank of the Seine would have certainly enabled General Hodges to cut off the larger part of Army Group B and to destroy it. This omission was the salvation of the German forces. The Fifth Panzer Army carried out its crossing at Rouen under unbelievable hardships, suffering heavy losses as the result of thousands of air sorties. Although most of their heavy weapons and vehicles fell into the hands of the enemy, it was an extraordinary military feat that they managed to cross the river at all, under the converging pressure of the attack and the dense barrage of artillery and aerial bombing. It required a high degree of steadfastness to take up the battle again on the north bank with improvised formations. The physical and mental strain on the troops was indeed great; their behavior was admirable. The Seine line could, of course, no longer be held, as Hitler had originally ordered.

The German High Command now intended to collect the Panzer divisions in the Beauvais-Compiègne area and regroup them for "a decisive blow at the flank of the enemy pushing across the Seine." This was a wishful dream which could not be realized, especially because barely a hundred tanks out of six Panzer divisions managed to assemble. A second and subsequent plan was to shift the Panzer formations to the area between the Marne and the Seine and use them for a southeastward push and relieve the pressure on the retreat of General Blaskowitz' Army Group G. This too was an illusion. If either operation were to succeed, the Seine line would have to be firmly held, and this was too much for the strength of the German forces in the west.

THE FALL OF PARIS

Before the German First Army had a chance to patch up its long front with security units and base personnel—stiffened only by combat troops of the 48th Division, part of the 338th Division, and a storm battalion—Patton's Third Army forced a crossing of the Seine between Melun and Fontainebleau and its advance units were reconnoitering as far ahead as Troyes.

Downstream from Paris the enemy was crossing to the north bank of the Seine on both sides of Mantes and was feeling forward toward Beauvais.

Army Group G was still involved in rearguard actions north of Orange.

There were no combat troops in Paris itself, only security units for the supply and administrative services. In the west and south just outside Paris an improvised brigade was stationed, but it was without heavy weapons and was valuable only for reconnaissance and guard duties.

On August 23 Army Group B received an order from Hitler to destroy the bridges and other important installations in Paris, "even if residential areas and artistic monuments are destroyed thereby." The Chief of the General Staff did not pass on this order; but the Commandant of Greater Paris, General von Choltitz, had received this order from the High Command through Western Headquarters.

Choltitz telephoned for instructions as to how Hitler's orders were to be carried out. The Chief of Staff, afraid that telephone calls were being monitored, answered that Choltitz should act in accordance with the situation as it appeared to him. He said that the Army Group had *not* passed this order on. He reminded General von Choltitz of the previous arrangements that had been made orally. The general did not permit the demolitions to be carried out, and thus the architectural splendors of the city were spared.

The French Second Armored Division of General Leclerc forced its way into Paris from the south on August 24. There were only isolated pockets of resistance and they did not hold out for long. General von Choltitz surrendered the city and was taken prisoner. It would perhaps have been tactically expedient to have evacuated the city earlier and withdrawn its entire garrison to the north. But the commandant might well have been hanged for such an action. As it was, Model started proceedings against Choltitz *in absentia* for cowardice after the city had been surrendered.

As soon the High Command learned that Paris was lost, Adolf Hitler ordered that all available heavy artillery, V bombs, and aircraft were to be directed against Paris. He thought of the destruction of Paris as a "moral weapon." Had these orders been carried out, many thousands of lives would have been lost and the *ville lumière* would have sustained irreplaceable damage to its many works of art.

There was no military justification for such an order, quite apart from other considerations. There could be no tactical or strategic purpose in defending the city, which no longer had any military value, as the Allies had crossed the Seine in strength both above and below Paris. Once the city had fallen, the heart of the city was of no tactical importance.

The Chief of Staff of Army Group B was able to prevent

these orders from being transmitted and executed, and thus thwarted Hitler's destructive intentions. Paris was saved from destruction at the last minute.

The events of the last weeks of August were like a raging torrent that nothing could stem. The German Fifteenth Army took over the western front between the Channel coast and Amiens; the Seventh Army brought together its remnants north of the Seine and tried to form a defense line between the Somme and the Oise with the aid of the 275th Infantry Division, lent by the Fifteenth Army; the Fifth Panzer Army covered the retreat from the Seine to the Somme.

The British 1st Guard Armored Division succeeded in breaking through to Amiens and on August 30 in Saleux captured the commander of the Seventh Army, General Eberbach, while he was taking over command from the commander of the Fifth Panzer Army, SS Chief Group Leader Sepp Dietrich. Dietrich and Colonel von Gersdorff, Chief of Staff of the Seventh Army, just managed to escape. Infantry General Brandenberger took over command of the Seventh Army several days later.

The avalanche rolled onward and carried everything along with it.

Part of Army Group B had held out bravely in the Compiègne-Soissons area. Here, too, the Allies succeeded in breaking through on August 28 and bombarded the Army Group headquarters with tank and artillery fire. The headquarters was moved to the Château of Havrincourt, west of Cambrai.

The Allies stood at the Somme, the Aisne, and the Marne near Chalôns. The coastal "fortresses" were being surrounded one after another.

After the staff of Army Group B had reached its new

headquarters, a directive was received from the High Command on future strategy. The idea of defending "every foot of ground" was at last abandoned. The directive ordered that resistance was not to be so prolonged that it led to encirclement. Units must preserve their fighting strength. The armies were "to fight their way back"—in other words, to be pushed back by the enemy—to a new line from the Scheldt bridgehead at Breskens, over Antwerp, the Albert Canal, Hasselt, west of Maastricht, the Meuse, the western edge of the Argonne plateau to Langres, joining there with Army Group G, which would hold the line from Châlons-sur-Saône to the Swiss frontier. This new line, the High Command insisted, was to be held "at all costs."

But an orderly retreat had become impossible. The Allied motorized armies surrounded the slow and exhausted German divisions marching in separate groups, and smashed them. There was a jam of retreating German formations at Mons and considerable numbers were destroyed by the Allied armored units which overtook them. Weakened remnants of the Fifth Panzer and Seventh armies reached the Meuse on September 5. Out of all the Panzer units only some 100 tanks and units of self-propelled artillery crossed the river. Only the steadiness of the troops and the energy of their commanders permitted any resistance at all to be offered. From Army Group Headquarters to company command post, every commander had to fight in close contact with the enemy and every means of improvisation was used to compel a short halt in the enemy advance.

The Fifteenth Army managed to cross the Scheldt with the majority of its units and with its heavy equipment intact. Of course the Fifteenth had not been so hard pressed by the enemy as other armies.

It was not possible to hold the Meuse line for long; Namur had fallen on September 6 and Liége on September 8. The former "fortresses" could not be defended, for lack of troops.

Then a new directive came from the High Command. It demanded delaying actions so that the Westwall could be fortified. The final line that was to be held "to the last man" was the Dutch coast and the mouth of the Scheldt, the Westwall as far as Luxembourg, and the western frontiers of Lorraine and Alsace.

Then something unexpected occurred, a German variation of the "miracle of the Marne" for the French in 1914: the furious advance of the Allies suddenly subsided. The reason could not have been serious supply difficulties, with such secure and undisturbed lines of communication. Nor was the reason the "declining momentum of the attack," as new full-strength formations were being continually brought up. The methodical tactics of the Allied Supreme Command must be considered the main reason. Perhaps the imaginary strength implied in the name "Westwall" still impressed the enemy. The enemy spread out and made preparations to overcome this supposed fortified line. Had the Allies kept up the attack on their enemy, they could have pursued the German forces until they "dropped from exhaustion," and could have ended the war half a year earlier. There were no longer any German ground forces worth mentioning in existence, to say nothing of air forces. Moreover, the battles in East Prussia and Hungary had reached a climax, and no forces could be released for the western front.

The Chief of Staff of Army Group B was recalled without explanation on September 5 while at La Chaudefontaine, east of Liége, and was replaced by Infantry General Krebs. He was arrested on September 7 on Himmler's orders and taken to the cellars of the main Reich security office in Prinz Albrechtstrasse in Berlin.

During the short period when he served with Field Marshal Model, he had found ample opportunity to discuss the general situation with him and to mention the political and military measures which in his opinion ought to be taken. Model clearly saw the hopelessness of the total situation, especially because of foreign political events in the east and southeast: Turkey had gone over to the Allies; Rumania, Bulgaria, and Finland had reached agreements with them.

Model declined to speak to Hitler about these matters, which he called "none of my business." He also would not hear of independent strategic decisions in the west, although the army leaders and field commanders repeatedly urged such a decision. He reminded them of the trials that followed the mutiny of July 20.

It was useless to appeal to his sense of moral responsibility to the people, to posterity, and to the German military tradition. The worse the situation grew, the more Model sought the support of Germany's political leaders. Outward symptoms were his request that a National Socialist political officer be attached to Army Group B, which had until then been avoided, and that an SS officer be assigned as his aide-de-camp. No decisions of basic political or military importance could be expected from this commander. He was content to be responsible for obeying orders, and a "revolt of the conscience" was far from his mind.

THE DEATH
OF FIELD MARSHAL ROMMEL

MARSHAL ROMMEL had suffered severe injuries from the fighter attack of July 17. There were numerous shell fragments in his head, his left eye was injured and his skull was badly fractured, as well as his cheekbones and temples. He remained unconscious for a long time from severe concussion. When his Chief of Staff visited him on the morning of July 24 at the Luftwaffe Hospital in Bernay, he had regained full consciousness. He asked how the struggle at the front was going, how the troops were, and about the events of July 20. He discussed the political consequences, which to him seemed uncertain.

Rommel was moved to Le Vésinet Military Hospital near St. Germain when the breakthrough at Caen was imminent. Although a detailed report was made to the High Command and the German press, there were no newspaper or radio announcements regarding his injuries. Rommel was anxious that the public should know that he had been disabled since July 17, as Hitler was trying to make him responsible for the worsening situation in Normandy.

After the Avranches breakthrough—three weeks later—an undated announcement was published and broadcast about Marshal Rommel's "automobile accident." Then there was silence again. In vain the Marshal demanded a correction of the version of the incident which had been issued by the highest authority.

Rommel was moved on August 8, at his own request, to his home at Herrlingen, near Ulm on the Danube, to be under the care of his wife and two professors from Tübingen, Dr. Albrecht and Dr. Stock. This was the right prescription; he recovered with surprising rapidity in his home surroundings.

The Chief of Staff visited him for the last time on September 6, the day following his recall from Army Group B, and found him apparently active and well. The injured left eye was half open again. He hoped to have recovered in a month, or at least be able to move about. The Chief of Staff informed him of the situation and of his own recall, which was at the same time a warning to Rommel. Then they discussed in detail the revolt of July 20. Speaking of Hitler, the Marshal exclaimed: "That pathological liar has now gone completely mad. He is venting his sadism on the conspirators of July 20, and this won't be the end of it!"

He was tortured with the problem of finding a way out of the fast-developing catastrophic events that were overtaking Germany. There seemed to be little hope of finding an even somewhat acceptable solution, after the events of the early summer of 1944 and the failure of the July plot.

Rommel entrusted his Chief of Staff with a message to Colonel General Guderian, now Chief of the German General Staff, to whom he was to report on September 8 at the Führer's headquarters. Rommel wanted the war in the west to be ended under any reasonable conditions whatsoever.

It must be ended while the Westwall and the Rhine were still in German hands, and the furies of war still had only slightly touched the German homeland. All available forces should be thrown into the eastern front, where the winter just ahead would favor the Russian armies and, in the light of previous experiences, would give us much to fear. It was more than ever necessary to eliminate Hitler. He, Rommel, would not bow to the power of destiny. As soon as he was well he would be ready to fill the breach and accept responsibility of any kind.

Rommel said to his doctor a week before his death: "I am afraid that this madman will sacrifice the last German before he meets his own end."

The Field Marshal had been given many indications and reports in the past year that he was being watched by the Secret Police of the SS, particularly during his stay at Herrlingen. The police were supposed to have reported to Himmler as early as the spring of 1944 that Rommel was a defeatist.

Rommel visited his old friend and regimental comrade Lieutenant Colonel of the Reserves Oskar Farny on October 13 in Durren, near Wangen, in the Allgäu. When they met, Rommel said, "I am in grave danger. Hitler wants to do away with me. His reasons are my ultimatum to him on July 15, the open and honest opinions I have always expressed, the events of July 20, and the reports of the Party and the Secret Police. If anything should happen to me, I beg you to take care of my son."

When Farny protested that it would be impossible for psychological reasons for Hitler to put his most popular army leader on trial, Rommel replied: "You will see. He will have me put to death. You are a politician and should understand this criminal better than I. He won't be afraid to do this."

Here is the picture of the death of Field Marshal Rommel, as given by his wife, Lucie Maria Rommel, and witnesses who have been interrogated.

The Field Marshal was summoned by telephone to an "important conference in the Führer's headquarters" on October 7. Since his doctors felt that he was not able to travel, Generals Burgdorf and Maisel came to him instead at Herrlingen on October 14, on behalf of Hitler.

There was a short conversation between Burgdorf and the Field Marshal, after which Rommel went to his wife and said to her in a voice that seemed to come from another world: "I shall be dead in a quarter of an hour. Hitler has given me the choice of taking poison or appearing before the People's Court."

General Burgdorf had explained to him that he had been implicated by the testimony of arrested and convicted men as a participant in the revolt of July 20. It had even been planned for him to be chief of state after a successful revolt. Up to this time it is not clear how the Field Marshal reacted in the face of the detailed accusations, which he rejected. It is a fact that after this conference he took leave of his family and his adjutant, Captain Aldinger, and left the house with both generals.

The grounds of the house and all roads out of Herrlingen were guarded meanwhile by SS guards with machine guns. Rommel was taken away in a car driven by an SS man, and soon after, his dead body was delivered by the two generals to the Army Reserve Hospital at the Wagner School in Ulm.

General Burgdorf forbade Dr. Meyer, the chief doctor of the hospital, to make an autopsy. "Do not touch the corpse," he said; "everything has already been arranged in Berlin."

They told his wife that the Field Marshal had died from

an embolism. The face of the dead Field Marshal wore an expression of extreme disdain.

Whatever the cause of this Shakespearean end, it is certain from the testimony of Marshal Keitel in Nuremberg that Burgdorf received his orders directly from Hitler, and that the fictitious story of an embolism was maintained by Hitler even to such close associates as Göring, Dönitz, and Jodl.

The telegram sent to Army Group B read: "Field Marshal Rommel has died from the effects of the automobile accident." If this death sentence, like that of Socrates, were executed by his own hand—although he had said to Mrs. Farny on October 13, "If anything should ever happen to me, never believe that I have raised my hand against myself"—Rommel would have regarded it both as a sacrifice and as an appeal to the conscience of the German people. Hitler sought to camouflage his deed and cover its traces by ordering a state funeral on October 18 in the city hall of Ulm, which was a political desecration of the dead without precedent in history. Neither he nor any other personage of the Party hierarchy appeared at the burial service. Only the Chief of the Reich Security Office, Dr. Kaltenbrunner, personally witnessed the ceremony. Counsellor Dr. Berndt of the Reich Propaganda Ministry said to Frau Rommel afterward, in portentous tones, "The Reichsführer of the SS has had no part in this. He is most deeply moved."

Field Marshal von Rundstedt had been detailed to represent Hitler, and read a speech that contained the pathetic words: "His heart belonged to the Führer!"

He took no part in the cremation which immediately followed, nor did he enter the house of mourning at Herrlingen. The old soldier appeared to those present to be broken and bewildered.

Some months after the funeral, Frau Rommel received the following letter from the Architect in Chief for German Warriors' Cemeteries, dated March 7, 1945.

My dear Frau Rommel,

The Führer has assigned me to erect the monument to your late husband, Field Marshal Erwin Rommel, and in accordance with his wishes I have requested several sculptors to work with me in creating designs for this memorial. As it is not possible at the present moment either to build it to full size or to transport it, it will be produced only on the scale of a model. But it is appropriate to place a simpler memorial on the grave now, in the form of a large stone tablet with the name and emblems inscribed on it. This slab will be approximately three feet wide and six feet long. The highest decoration awarded to the Field Marshal will be engraved over the inscription.

I thought it right to commemorate the heroism and greatness of the Field Marshal in the form of a lion. Professor Thorak has modeled a dying lion, Professor Breker a roaring lion, and sculptor Löhner a lion rampant. I have chosen the third design for the medallion on the slab, as, in my opinion, it will show up best. But if you should prefer it, the stone can just as well bear the dying lion as modeled by Professor Thorak and sketched on one of these reproductions.

This gravestone can be prepared immediately, as I have obtained special permission from Reich Minister Speer, although at the moment stone monuments in general are not permitted for anyone, including soldiers and even Knights of the Iron Cross. I have obtained special permission to work on and erect such memorials in exceptional cases and will, if you allow me, use it for the first time for the gravestone of the hero Rommel, so that it can be placed on the grave within a short time.

Heil Hitler!
(signed) Dr. Kreis
Chief Architect

But among the people and his soldiers, the word still went from mouth to mouth: "He murdered him."

Hitler's reasons for the elimination of Rommel go back to the time of the African campaign, and especially to the events of the early summer of 1944.

One of Goebbels' stories published in the weekly magazine *Das Reich* once described Rommel as one of the first SA leaders. Rommel had never left the Army and could therefore never have been in the SA. The story may have had its origin in his activities in 1936, when he was a liaison officer of the High Command of the Army to the Reich Youth Leader and advised on premilitary youth training. As a battalion commander in Goslar during the first two years of National Socialist rule, Rommel was inwardly opposed to Hitler. He remarked to his friend Oskar Farny after the lawless acts of June 30, 1934, and especially after the unpunished shooting of Generals von Schleicher and von Bredow: "Now would have been a good time to throw out Hitler and his whole gang."

Rommel began to respect and honor Hitler after March 1935, when Hitler proclaimed the end to the arms limitation. Rommel saw him as the "unifier of the nation," which had been torn apart by the many parties, the "liberator" from the unworthy clauses of the Versailles treaty, and the "eliminator of unemployment." He began to believe in the "peaceful aims and ideals" of Hitler and was impressed by his co-ordinating powers. Rommel welcomed the 1935 proclamation as a sign of the restitution of the sovereignty of the Reich. He believed that the Western powers would welcome German rearmament as a "buffer against Bolshevism."

Rommel did not at first perceive that war is not only a military but also a political process. But after the end of the western campaign of 1940, he began to doubt the states-

manship and war leadership of the National Socialist regime. Many bitter experiences confirmed these doubts. At
El Alamein and afterward, Rommel for the first time con-
tradicted Hitler's pipe dream of world domination. Hitler's
distrust dates from that time, but he still wanted to make
capital for himself with the German people out of the re-
spectability of Rommel, and for that reason gave him more
publicity than any other general. He was all the more
willing to do this since he thought he could use the experienced field soldier as a counterweight to the hated
General Staff.

Rommel's understanding of military and political affairs
grew, as did his understanding of humanity. He recog-
nized the growing amorality of the regime that made the
state and the armed forces subordinate to the Party. Time
and again he protested against the corruption of the jurid-
ical system which seemed to him to be the shortest way to
the destruction of the state. As the mistakes and crimes of
Hitler in all realms mounted, Rommel shuddered at the
terrible power of the monster—"that accumulation of senseless greed in its most brutal form; desire for renown; the
conqueror's dream of power; lust for killing and destruction; vainglory and paralyzing fear; thirst for vengeance;
and boundless despair."

Rommel, as he saw these terrible manifestations, did not
resign himself to inactivity, as some of the senior officers
did. Rather, this awareness developed in him a resiliency
of mind and heart which prepared him for independent
action. He was not only courageous with his pen, but also
when face to face with Hitler. He was unsparing in revealing the situation as it really was and in demanding that the
necessary measures be taken. Knowing that his protesta-
tions were unsuccessful, but feeling that the reputation
and the life of his people meant more than his own, he

got ready to strike a blow such as Yorck's. Ernst Jünger's words fit Marshal Rommel:

There are situations in which you must ignore the chances of success; then you stand above politics. That is true of these men, and therefore morally they triumphed although historically they failed. Their courage and sacrifice was of a higher nature than the battlefield can produce, and although victory did not crown them, poetry will.

Rommel's comprehension and decision came late. The conscience of the soldier developed only slowly into a political one, and then moved toward the spiritual. He began to grasp Jünger's ideas of peace, and he looked upon a new world and guessed at the mysterious interrelationship of faith and reality.

But when he was about to act, destiny intervened. Rommel, like most other high officers, did not participate in creating the glorification of "the greatest general of all time." Hitler instinctively discerned the attitude of Rommel; he had proof of it during their encounter on June 17 at the Margival conference. Hitler was openly and covertly influenced against Rommel by his entourage, Keitel, Burgdorf and others. The general must not become a menace to the dictator. There must be no other national hero in this theocracy built around Hitler.

The revolt of July 20, 1944, gave him the opportunity he desired to rid himself of his only rival and possible successor. The hatred of the people was channeled by German propaganda in a masterly fashion and it drew their attention away from the impending catastrophe. There was to be no one in Germany who could take Hitler's place. Rommel was the most popular man during the war, for his human qualities as well as for his military successes. He was willing to spring into the breach and avert chaos. Hitler probably would not have dared to put Rommel before a court in the autumn of 1944. Whatever decision the Field Marshal had made in the noon hour of October 14 at Herrlingen, he would never have reached Berlin or Hitler's headquarters alive.

Incidentally, interrogations after the war made it plain that Rommel's intentions were not known in detail to Himmler and his henchmen.

Murder was the only political weapon that Hitler could use to gain his ends without revealing his own weakness. To conceal it with a state funeral was merely a refinement of the reign of terror.

Niccolo Machiavelli wrote four hundred years ago: The general whose skill has brought victory and success to the Prince, must stand in such high esteem with the soldiers, the people and the enemy, that the Prince must not merely be grateful for victories. The Prince must secure himself against his general, do away with him, or strip him of his renown.

vi

ERWIN ROMMEL
AS A SOLDIER

THE FIELD MARSHAL

ACCORDING to Clausewitz, the man who would become a general must have high intellectual gifts combined with "strength of will" and a "courageous spirit." "Every operation," he said, "has to be guided by one single clear and simple thought."

Rommel's book *Infantry in Attack* gives sufficient evidence of his gift for reducing the complexities of minor tactics to a simple formula. He applied the same talent to the art of commanding medium-sized and large armies.

Strategic planning and command were further from his realm than technical and tactical problems; these latter he mastered with his innate gift for making complicated matters seem simple.

He demanded clarity in the estimation of practical possibilities and accuracy in reporting what had been done. He hated propagandistic embellishment and the exaggerations that as a result of political pressure found their way into the official language of the Wehrmacht after 1941. In spite of this, he himself succumbed at times to the thesis that propaganda is necessary in war.

The Field Marshal had intuition, the ability to see all at a glance on the battlefield. He did not merely follow a plan worked out in advance, but made adjustments according to "events and circumstances." He was a master of improvisation because of his instinctive insight and his powers of decision. His imagination was lively with practical and technical ideas.

The enemy praised the "flair" of the "Desert Fox" in the African campaign. Churchill in Parliament explained the severe British reverses in North Africa with the words: "There was a great general fighting against us." A Gallup poll in 1942 designated him as the most important and most clever general. Thus his renown spread throughout the world.

Rommel had the steadfastness that is necessary for any commander who inevitably is subject to sudden changes of fortune and who must master successive crises in battle. His sound perception saved him from delusions in military matters and gave him the right feeling for the point of culmination in a battle, or the climax in a war.

Moltke demanded a "balance between authority and confidence." Although Rommel tended to demand too much and could be overly severe, he had the genius of leadership, the gift of inspiring the troops, that legendary influence that the great leader exerts upon his men which cannot be explained logically. The soldiers sensed the depth of his manly qualities and the pulse of the great heart that beat for them. The Field Marshal could thus dominate both mind and matter.

It was so even in 1915 in the Argonne, when Lieutenant Rommel took command of the adjoining company in the adjacent sector. One felt as much confidence in him then as in the second World War when his "Phantom" division tore across France or when his Afrika Korps dashed across the African desert of El Alamein and Tobruk. "The front is where Rommel is," the troops said. "You cannot command an army from the Tuileries," said Napoleon. This admonition is true also in the age of advanced technology. Rommel was a modern "Marshal Forward," who formed the link between the advance command post and the necessarily more remote headquarters. He was tireless, and was to be found wherever the troops needed his infectious presence. He loved the ever changing life of the soldier, the incessant movement, the rigorous life, and the magnetic tensions that grip all soldiers. Hitler was devoid of such harmony with the troops and lacked what Rommel possessed—the art of handling men and the power of commanding troops that Schiller's Max Piccolomini praises in *Wallenstein:*

> He draweth out the strength of every man,
> Peculiar to his task, enlarges it,
> Yet keepeth every man just what he is,
> Ensuring that he ever so maintains
> His proper place. Thus he unites
> The powers of all his soldiers with his own.

THE MAN

Count Schlieffen required of a general that intellect, heart, and will power culminate in character: *non videri, sed esse*—be rather than seem. In the encounter between reason and the irrational forces of war, in the balance between knowledge and action, the man emerges from the general. The Field Marshal always remained "the selfsame Rommel," doing his duty even in the most adverse circumstances—a soldier with "civil courage," whose love of his country was founded upon truth and rooted in his native soil and in timeless nature. Candid and frank, honest with friend and enemy, he was a man who was inwardly free. He considered honorable whatever his conscience permitted. His clear blue eyes and warm animated face, humane for all its appearance of energy and boldness, inspired confidence. He was hard on himself, of Spartan habits, and yet he did not despise the pleasures of life. He was not given to meditation, and it was late in his life that he gained an understanding of the most fundamental things. Sometimes he seemed cool and reserved, but with those he knew well he could be a good comrade and displayed a pleasant sense of humor.

From his Swabian origin there sprang a deep social conscience. His chivalry was proverbial and lives in many stories. The enemy respected this "dashing general."

Erwin Rommel, a *miles fati*, remains the personification of the good and decent in the German soldier. His life and works are throughout, a manly and humane legacy left to his country for all time.

vii

OBSERVATIONS ON THE
BATTLE OF NORMANDY

T HE WESTERN ALLIES regarded the invasion of Normandy as an operation that would decide the whole
war. Their preparations for it went back as far as mid-1942.
The technical preparations were extraordinary both with
respect to inventiveness and execution. The Allies actually
worked out with mathematical exactitude how much could
be left to chance. The inventors and engineers of two
hemispheres succeeded in accomplishing feats that had previously been thought impossible. Artificial harbors made
landing operations and supply independent of the capture
of French ports. Nothing more advantageous than the pipe-
line "Pluto," which carried fuel under the Channel waters,
could have been thought of. The expendable wealth of
the outside world could be utilized for these achievements.
Artificial landing strips on improvised airfields in the
bridgeheads made possible the closest co-operation between
the air forces and the army and naval units.

The Allies had all the advantages in close- and long-

range reconnaissance during the years of preparation for
the invasion. For the Germans the wireless services were
almost the only effective source of information, whereas
the Allies used their air supremacy to good advantage.
They combined bombing behind the German front with
their reconnaissance missions, both of which they thought
essential for the success of the invasion.

The British and Americans had at their disposal an established and well-trained world-wide intelligence service. In
the invasion areas they also used the forces of the resistance
in the occupied countries, which supplied them with the
necessary details about German fighting strength and kept
them constantly up to date.

Before the war Hitler had forbidden any preparations
for building up an intelligence service in Great Britain.
When, at the last moment, it was attempted to establish
such a system, it was too late.

The Americans and British had an overwhelming superiority on land and sea and in the air. Their air forces
were technically highly developed and well trained and
commanded; these air forces were the decisive factor for
the Allied victories in the invasion and subsequent operations. The air-ground co-operation was rehearsed to the
last detail, and it must be acknowledged that it stood every
test in practice. To this it must be added that the Allied
ground forces were equipped with excellent weapons,
were exceptionally well supplied, and were highly mobile.
The British and American divisions started the invasion
with their strength undiminished by warfare, and were
carefully trained on the basis of the lessons learned during
five years of war. The German Army, in contrast, had behind it the campaigns in Poland, Norway, France, Africa,
Italy, the Balkans, and Russia; it had bled itself white and
was exhausted. It was undernourished; its supplies were

inadequate. The winter of Stalingrad had inflicted some half a million irreplaceable casualties and had broken the back of the German Army.

The power of the Luftwaffe had been consumed by the Battle of Britain, and its subsequent development did not keep step with modern requirements.

The words of Clausewitz on the moral greatness of a cause in war can be applied to the Allies. "The material forces seem only to be the wooden scabbard," he wrote; "the moral forces are the noble metal, the sharp and gleaming sword." The moral strength of the Allied cause was greater than that of the German. The transgressions of Hitler had created a moral vacuum. The purely military leadership of the Allies lagged behind their amazing technical preparations and achievements. They succeeded best in matters of organization and leadership, particularly in the co-ordination and command of the three services. There is hardly a case in history that shows less of the inevitable friction and tension between allies in a coalition than appeared in the military leadership in the invasion of Normandy.

The Allied leadership on the continent was tactically and strategically methodical. It complied wtih Marshal Foch's insistence upon *"sûreté de la manœuvre,"* and it sought to eliminate every risk, keep casualties down to a minimum, and put into practice the attack *à coup sûr*.

The Allied armies therefore resembled a rigid line that pushed their enemy backward, like a steamroller that was slowly but surely to crush him.

The Allied command repeated its mistakes of the North African landings of 1942 in failing to exploit fully its great strategic opportunities; otherwise the war would have ended in 1944. As examples of missed opportunities one might mention the failure to roll back the Seine front after

the battle of the Falaise pocket, and the failure to break
through the Westwall and strike across the Rhine into the
interior of Germany in September 1944. General Patton,
under General Bradley's command, was the only Allied
general who dared exceed the limits of safety with his army
in the endeavor to carry out large-scale operations; but he
could not impart his impetus to the over-all Allied command, and he earned little thanks for his generalship.

These observations do not alter the importance of the
invasion to the slightest degree; it broke up the German
front in the west and rolled it back. It took so much pressure off the Soviet Union that it made possible the successes
of the Red Army in 1944 and 1945. The technical support
of the United States played a part in those victories too—
the Russian heavy T-34 tank was powered by American
engines. The United States was producing two thousand
tanks per month merely for her own use even before the
invasion began.

The invasion of Normandy will forever remain an event
of the first order in the history of war. It was the first big
operation to succeed fully in bringing together and leading
the forces of all three services to attain one strategic goal.

The German High Command did not take the necessary
steps to adapt its structure to the need for combined operations on land and sea and in the air.

The "war lord" Adolf Hitler thought in terms of the
Continent and was enmeshed in memories of the static fronts
of the first World War. A war of all three services against
the whole world, with the heavy demands for equipment
for land and air warfare, simply overtaxed the industrial
and technical resources of Germany. This Hitler did not
want to admit. Divisions dependent on horses for transport,
of the type used in the first World War, had to fight a

mechanized enemy; sixty out-of-date divisions were not enough to "defend" the entire length of 2,500 miles of foreign coasts and frontiers. An "air force" consisting, at the beginning of the invasion, of ninety fighters and seventy bombers was supposed to maintain supremacy of the air, to reconnoiter, and to afford close support for the ground forces. The High Command was forced to issue an order early in 1944 that "every airplane in the sky is to be considered hostile."

Unscrupulousness was balanced by amateurishness in the German Supreme Command.

The Führer and the High Command of the Armed Forces directed operations from Berchtesgaden in the first weeks of the invasion, and then from East Prussia. There were grave disadvantages in these distances, particularly as air communication was impossible—as grave in fact as those that hampered the much criticized German High Command in Luxembourg during the 1914 Battle of the Marne. No German leader came to the Normandy front; on the Allied side, Winston Churchill was among the first to visit the Continent after the invasion. The chaos in the chain of command, resulting from the struggle between Army and Party leaders—sharply contrasting with the "leadership principle"— hampered any attempt to give clear-cut orders and led to divided authority. It was the soldier at the front who paid the price.

Instead of confidence between officers and men, there was compulsion, falsehood, political trials, and courts-martial. There was no more of that eagerness among junior officers to accept responsibility and take the initiative that was once the trademark of the German soldier. As things stood, and taking into consideration the comparative strength of the opponents—quite apart from political solutions—only large-scale strategy could have offered hope of salvation. Instead, fighting went on simultaneously in all theaters of war. Strategic decisions made at the proper time would have averted the most annihilating blows of the enemy: in the east, the front should have been drastically shortened and strengthened, and a strong reserve built up; in the south, there should have been withdrawal to the Pisa-Florence-Adria line and then to the line of the Alps; in the west, first of all, France south of the Seine should have been abandoned, a striking force formed on the eastern flank, and forethought given to rearward lines which could receive the retreating troops and could then be defended.

But Hitler, unable to compromise politically or in his propaganda, devoid of any sober clarity of thought, ordered the troops to hold their ground at any cost and abandoned 200,000 men in his "fortresses." The fighting man was thus physically, spiritually, and morally overburdened. There began a bleeding of the German Army similar to that which took place in the Russian winter of 1942–43. The defensive war had to be fought without adequate firepower and without the support of the other two services— it was a beggars' war.

As for the technical conduct of operations, Hitler was not accustomed to give long-range orders. He issued piecemeal tactical orders and often interfered on even the lowest levels of command. Usually his orders were not applicable to the situation by the time they were received. There could never be that degree of confidence in him that the strain of battle demanded; his methods ignored the dignity of the soldier and of the human being.

The war on the western front in the summer of 1944 must have cost Germany half a million casualties, including those trapped in the fortress areas. The losses of matériel cannot be estimated. There were only 40,000 dead in the west in the campaign of 1940.

In the western campaign Hitler was unable to perceive the moment of climax. He deceived others, but he deceived himself most terribly of all, when he tried to veil the inescapable facts and raise false hopes in his "miracle weapons," instead of recognizing Germany's actual position and drawing the necessary political consequences therefrom.

Even as late as 1944, Hitler completely underestimated his enemies in the west. "No clever fighter disdains his foe," says Goethe in *Iphigenie*. Hitler lived in a world of fantasy without any sense of proportion, exaggerating his own will power and possessed by delusions of grandeur. He spilled the life blood of the nation both by his authoritarian methods of defense and by such offensive operations on the Normandy front as the Avranches counterattack.

An army ceases to be an army when it is incapable of fighting. Whenever this occurred in past wars, responsible military and political leaders drew the appropriate conclusions. One might recall the action of France to end the war of 1870–71, and the decisions of Hindenburg and Ludendorff to end the first World War in the autumn of 1918.

This weighty decision was again necessary in the summer of 1944. Soldiers conscious of their responsibilities— among them Rommel—tried to remove Hitler and bring the war to an end. Thus the revolt of July 20 was attempted, but it failed. There were no direct effects upon the front. The facts did not become known until much later; the motives, scope, and results of the revolt remained hidden from the ordinary fighting man.

Adolf Hitler consciously gave way to illusions by refusing to recognize that the war was lost. He put his hopes in the V-1, in U-boat warfare, in the collapse of the coali-

tion between Russia and the United States. He did not, and
did not wish to, draw the right conclusions.

Fateful tragedy overtook the German army. In perform-
ance and behavior the German divisions met Seeckt's re-
quirement "to possess icy courage and so withstand misfor-
tune."

It is the tragedy of every German soldier and of German
history that such courage was misused and sacrificed for a
phantom. Every German now suffers the disastrous consequences: hundreds of thousands of soldiers are still in
prison; hundreds of thousands have perished in obscurity;
their officers, if they did not die in battle, died by hanging
or by suicide; others remain prisoners of war or live like
beggars in their own country. Those who returned home
found a ruined fatherland crowded with millions of refu-
gees and expellees.

But if there is to be true peace, justice must be done to
all men, even to the conquered and to the millions who
died. In the words of Karl Jaspers:

He who is conscious of his honor as a soldier is untarnished
by the many discussions of war guilt. He who has been faith-
ful to his comrades, unswerving in danger, courageous and objective, may retain something inviolable in his conscience. All
nations honor this conduct which is at the same time both
soldierly and human. This is proof of the very meaning of life.

A purified Germany and a new unified Europe in a
peaceful world cannot exist without this indisputable concept, from which all soldiers in the past have drawn their
strength and to which the best have given their lives.

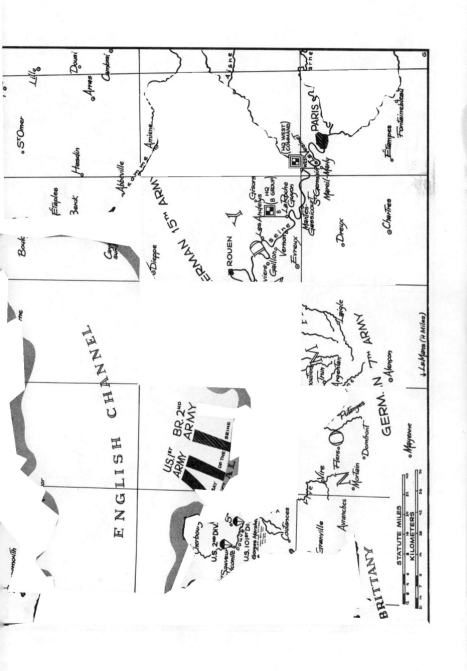

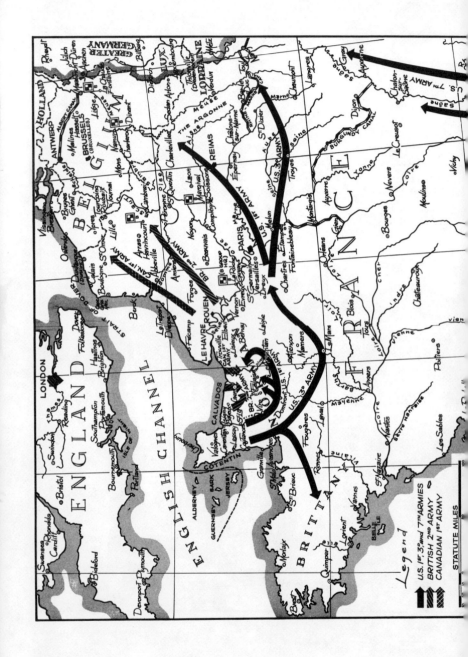